DEMONSAPIENISM®

&

TRUE COCK WORSHIP

LORDESS DEMONICA™

Papilio Publishing Co.
PO Box 18595
INDIAN SPRINGS NV 89018-0139

Book Disclaimer

Do not purchase or read this book if you are:

- Easily offended by a belief that is unlike your own
- Sensitive to graphic and/or sexual content that might be disturbing
- Unable to accept that people are entitled to freedom of speech under the rights of the United States First Amendment.

ISBN-10 0-615-43850-4
ISBN-13 9780615438504

DEMONSAPIENISM & TRUE COCK WORSHIP
Copyright © 2011 Lordess Demonica

Printed in the United States of America

Dedications of this book are for those that are willing to come forward and proudly represent their demonic lineage. May you always have the sub-deity in your heart through the love of True Cock Worship or forever keep masturbating as Demonsapienists. This book is my resume to God that Shem might be pleased with my work.

Thank you Stacy Darlene for helping edit this book and Randall Connor for being such a good listener and lover.

CONTENTS

PREFACE

For centuries, the word worship has been defined as one's personal beliefs and/or devotion to a deity. In the last decade, the porn industry has recklessly exploited this word and its original meaning. Other types of worship now come in a multitude of subdivisions. According to the porn industry, worship is anything for which people have an erotic fetish, such as muscle, foot and breast worship.

True Cock Worship is a small but growing subculture in the United States consisting of individuals who believe the penis to be a deity. They respect the original meaning of the word "worship." They live a life of commitment by worshiping the penis through prayer, meditation and oral sex. Traditional religions do not accept them and believe them to be possessed by demons. These individuals are also misunderstood and mocked in the BDSM community. True Cock Worshipers are attacked from both sides of the spectrum due to their eccentric mindset by not conforming to traditions.

Historical evidence shows that various parts of Africa, South America, Europe and Asia have their own interpretations of spiritual cock worship. The United States has little history in regards to it; however, there is a great respect for the philosophies of the aforementioned continents. True Cock Worship from the western hemisphere is not an extension nor is it affiliated with any particular faith. Such underground cults in America might incorporate sexuality with their beliefs but not solely for the penis as with True Cock Worship.

True Cock Worshipers are very passionate about their faith. Exploring one's own sexuality through God is a part of being true to one's self. Gender is defined as whatever one's will destines them to be. It is pertinent that all of us learn to embrace human sexuality while not being hindered by religious conformity. All can achieve a fulfilling sense of peace in this life with an open mind as long as we are unbiased. Penis worship is for one's ultimate blessings and spiritual exaltation. This is the sacred belief of a True Cock Worshiper.

Chapter 1
PHILOSOPHY OF TRUE INTELLIGENCE

There is a divine progression of enlightenment enabling humanity the ability to receive spiritual knowledge through an intellectual path. Being intelligent is important for some of us. As sad as it may be, most individuals will take the easy route by riding on the intelligence of another human's ideas. Humanity is too lazy, afraid, or does not have the faith to pursue its own intellectual path.

Demonsapienists believe that less than 10 percent of human beings will never bother to discover their own intellectual path. Although discovering one's intellectual path is a possibility, few will seek it. The intellectual path that leads directly to God is the thread that brings mankind to a personal revelation or belief. Interestingly enough, individuals that have discovered their own path to God will find it to be unique compared to the paths of others, with a few exceptions. One might discover his or her own personal revelation while exchanging thoughts with other free thinkers. For example, a personal revelation might happen during a life after death experience.

Demonsapienists define true intelligence as having the ability to think apart from everyone else's belief or having a combination of inspired beliefs. True intelligence is identifiable by an exchange of words that expresses one's unique beliefs and/or concepts. Beliefs originate from individuals that can think for themselves. Those with personal revelations sometimes share their philosophy with other individuals that have no spiritual concept of their own.

Every so often, a demon prodigy arrives and becomes a special instrument on earth to enlighten other demons. These remarkable individuals become the key to life for all if not most humans. Demonic prodigies that come and go are the seeds to knowledge and possess the unique ability to convince the world to believe in their brilliant concepts.

Demonsapienists have demonic prodigies who we know as Galileo, Newton, Einstein and Darwin. Their theories have defined much about the world we live in by their own true intelligence. All of these demonic prodigies have discovered their own intellectual path, leading them to personal revelations about their own spirituality as well as human existence. Demonsapienists strongly believe in developing their own concepts while others have spiritual beliefs through religious conformity.

The whole mission in this life is to find the spiritual path that works best for you. Knowledge that does not come from one's personal revelation, becomes the reinvented knowledge that most demons depend on. If individuals cannot find what works by their own insight, then they will always be prone to following someone else's. Discovering your personal revelation first occurs through pursuing the intellectual path. A personal revelation is the only unique gift that sets apart your spiritual identity from the rest. True intelligence is the position that most demonsapiens avoid out of fear.

Honest demons are able to admit that fear is a demonic decision, and it can hinder a demon from opening himself up to his or her own spiritual enlightenment. The only true spiritual path is your own, and it can change if one allows it. Others can follow their own personal revelation or the revelation where God is depicted as being a dominant male entity and having a beard.

When demonsapiens build their belief system solely on the knowledge that comes from another demon, it is demonic pollution. Personal revelations are not demonic pollutions because they come without corruption from others.

God is a spiritual structure. To become one with God, we need to find our own personal revelation through our own true intelligence. Demons, also known as people, cannot be any less spiritually structured than God can. Our spiritual structure is in no way able to amount to the magnitude of God but in order to know God we have to exercise our own spiritual structure.

Some demonsapiens believe that someday we will be unified by one belief. Demonsapienists believe that individuals will discover God by understanding and applying one of two distinctive concepts of Demonsapienism (True Intelligence or True Cock Worship). It is unknown the amount of centuries it will take to unify the world, but true intelligence is expected to take hold in due time. Demonsapienism will be the start of true intelligence and personal revelations across the globe. The worst-case scenario will be that atheism will result from each personal revelation. Exchanging philosophies without bloodshed is feasible only if using the teachings and practices of Demonsapienism as a guide.

One with true intelligence is wasting his or her time with any individual that cannot identify the meaning of a personal revelation. Demonsapienists, also known as free thinkers, avoid spiritual corruption by not listening to demonic pollution. They prefer to share thoughts and ideas with other free thinkers that appreciate the uniqueness of another's philosophy.

Individuals who do not have the ability to use true intelligence or discover their own intellectual path are called "hoes." They only have the ability to study the philosophy of dead and/or living individuals and quote them. Hoes appear highly intellectual, however, they have very little or no substance and will argue anything based on what they have seen, read or heard. They are quick to debate any non-accredited philosophy that does not make sense to them. The common demonsapien (born in their right mind) is a philosopher. Hoes, however, will not agree with this viewpoint because they do not have true intelligence of their own.

Since the beginning of time, hoes have debated with free thinkers by paying institutions, universities and colleges to study the philosophies of other demonsapiens such as Socrates, Aristotle, Rene Descartes, Confucius, Avicenna and John Locke. They are motivated solely by demonic pollution and build their belief system solely upon the knowledge that comes from another individual. This kind of demonsapien has what is called a weak surface. This term might apply to every aspect of life, but it mostly defines individuals that have a faith that comes from someone or somewhere else.

It is not impressive nor is it true intelligence to quote and refer to books written by other individuals. A demonsapien's ability to express and share his or her own intellectual path rather than live through another demonsapien is most impressive. Demonsapienist can see right through hoes and usually try to avoid confrontations with them.

Walking into darkness is usually what many would call an individual that leaves the faith they were brought up with. Judgment will happen to anyone who discovers his or her intellectual path regardless of whether it is a demonic right. Unfortunately, hoes will never truly know themselves as long as they do not have a personal revelation of their own.

A personal revelation only comes from deep within. It can tie in to the spiritual philosophy of Demonsapienism or become unique. A free thinker that happens to agree with the concept (all people are demons) is automatically granted the right to be called a Demonsapienist.

Free thinkers do not have to agree with the originator of Demonsapienism because it is their right. In most cases, they already have discovered a path for themselves. Free thinkers that have yet to pursue their intellectual paths by receiving a personal revelation are encouraged to do so and should never turn away from what they discover. Every bit of consciousness is a personal revelation, whether it is right or wrong for someone else.

Chapter 2
PHILOSOPHY OF DEMONSAPIENISM

That we as demons are purely disillusioned by reality and choose to view ourselves as good, law-abiding citizens is understandable. For the most part, we are in denial about anything that would make us a classic indication of demonic unruliness. To hear someone openly refer to the demons of his or her dark past is common enough. Some individuals will brag openly about having faced their demons. This usually is interpreted as confronting one's fears and/or overcoming a difficult time. Honest demonsapiens will view this as the self-realization of coming to terms with their ugly character.

There are an unspoken number of individuals who believe we were all born as demons. A Demonsapienist is an individual that believes all people are demons and reside on earth in the embodiment of homo sapiens.

Demonsapienism is the belief that we all come from demonic lineage and are only civilized by cultured suppression. This concept allows anyone to have the authority to incorporate how they want to interpret spirituality, sex, science and philosophy through their own personal revelation. Demonsapienism encourages individuals to independently self-reflect and self explore everything in this life and beyond. It also has a foundation of its own that demonsapien followers use as a guide to dealing with life.

Some individuals believe that demons are fictional characters while others believe that they are real. True Cock Worshipers believe that demons are real and live as Demonsapienists. Other groups that believe in demons have a different perspective about them but from a traditional and religious standpoint.

For example, there are cults that originate in North America that claims particular ethnicities among us are demons. White Americans, from the Church of Latter Day Saints, have labeled all blacks as demons. African Americans, from the Nation of Islam, have labeled all whites as demons. What makes these theories ironic is both organizations are partially correct, however, both fail to realize that they too are demons.

Being referred to as a demon is not an easy concept to fathom nor is it an easy pill to swallow. Not many of us will want to come to terms with this concept. Indeed, most individuals will not until after the body is shed by death and our true essence is revealed. We then will come to the realization that our bodies were on lease.

Demonsapienists believe that no one is 100 percent sure about demonic existence, but we all have a right to our own thought process. It is our right to challenge religious scholars and those with degrees specializing in Demonology. They are nothing more than demonsapiens sharing thoughts with other demonsapiens. Possessing one's own thoughts is a right that can be shared, even if the view is ridiculous.

That all individuals gain knowledge about Demonology to understand how others choose to define demons is recommended. Furthermore, take what you have learned with a grain of salt, as you will need to have an open mind to appreciate the philosophy of Demonsapienism.

Demonsapienism provides the mental tools for individuals to live in the way that allows them to connect with God spiritually, sexually and intellectually. It also teaches servants of God how to live a balanced life in order to engage with demons successfully. Their mission is to lift up or tear down the mentality of another demonsapien in order to have a personal relationship with the penis.

There is no such thing as a mistake by God, according to Demonsapienism. Everything created is flawless and perfect, just as our imagination is unique like God's. The only part of creation that is not beautiful is the ugly picture that we as demons have painted for this world. This picture is the unavoidable ugly reality that many demonsapiens refuse to accept about themselves and to see in others.

For starters, the earth has had plenty of self-righteous demons that have chosen to entertain God by living ruthless. Some demonsapiens are pathetic for giving away their credibility and blaming the devil for their actions. Demonsapienists, however, do not believe that God created competition. There is no such entity as a fallen angel named Satan, Lucifer or the Devil fighting against the creator by influencing so-called "humans" to do evil. Believing in fallen angels that once turned against God is a concept created first by Judaism and then expanded greatly upon by Christianity.

Demonsapienists claim that there is an unsystematic power of chaos in the spirit world in which demons are given full and complete liberty to do anything and everything whether dead or alive. Servants of God do believe in angels but refer to them as the etkić. They do not believe in Archangels, however. Classifying demons by dividing them into honors and duties within a hierarchy does not exist in Demonsapienism. It is irrational to believe that all demons, the most ruthless of all God's creation, dwell in a controlled and structured system.

Demonsapienists furthermore do not support the belief that Archangels, also known as demons, have God-given names like Gabriel and Michael. The real name of a demon is actually mysterious because the earliest names began at the start of time. A name only can be determined by knowing how many times a demonsapien has returned to earth. Every nine generations a new name for the demon begins at birth then is added to go in front of their previous name.

God does not judge demonsapiens for things like lust and temptation. Judgment is what religions use as an excuse to justify wrong about a different belief. The God of this universe does not and has not ever punished any part of creation since temptation and lust is not a sin. Sin is not the word that Demonsapienists use to describe the lust that tempts them. There are various kinds of lust that narrow down to temptation. From one demon to the next, most forms of lust are nothing but repulsive. For example, lusting after another demon's job is one form of lust on an endless list of temptations. Lust will tempt us to do the ugliest things to harm one another.

Demonsapienists do at times refer to a phrase called demonic error, but it does not have anything to do with lust or temptation. Demonic error, for example, is a demon that might medically misdiagnose another demon out of carelessness. The result of demonic error would cause the ill demonsapien to die. Another example of demonic error would be a demonsapien driving home drunk and killing another demon's only child. Demonic errors are cases of recklessness that affect other demonsapiens based on acts of inconsideration and pure stupidity.

We call ourselves human, but we are as evil as it gets. It is therefore impossible for us to be possessed under these notions. Some demonsapiens are sweet, but generally we are all self-centered and ruthless. Some demonsapiens are nicer than others are but all are born narcissistic. It is therefore our nature to be rude, cold, selfish and greedy amongst other things.

Dwelling on earth as a saint is impossible because of the demonic mentality that we have from one demonic interaction to the next. We are God's most precious creation, but that does not grant anyone the right to be referred to as a saint. There is no such thing as a human interaction because all interactions are demonic interactions.

No one has ever walked the earth cleansed of demonic spirit. It is therefore impossible to dwell on earth as a perfect example to another human based on this logic. Kings, Queens, Saints, Priests, Pastors, Deacons, Messengers, Saviors, Messiahs, Leaders, Rulers, Dictators, and Presidents are no exception to the rule according to Demonsapienism. There is no such thing as pure and innocent with no character flaws.

"Humanity" is only a term that best describes a concept of denial. It is up to each individual to capture God's attention by demonstrating how intelligent a creation we are. We must continue discovering new ways of impressing our maker with positive ingenuity rather than negative hindrances. True Cock

Worshipers are less than pleasant demons who only want to do better in the eyes of God.

Although we have a government with laws that require us to conform, religion is ultimately what instills the difference from right and wrong. Many demons believe that we are here to impress God, and Demonsapienists agree. Some will try to apply the tools that is believed to please the Lord.

Some demons will struggle to find refuge and power over other demons. They will take leadership roles just to sabotage another demon's progress. The ones that follow have the least potential to impress God. These demons can be led to believe anything and are pathetic. They are the great majority of demons in our world. They are weak because they do not seek to impress God with their own thoughts. Demons born to lead are no more intelligent than demonsapiens that follow. The only characteristic that separates the two types of demons is courage.

The highest achievement known to all demonsapiens is encouraging others how to live for God by the use of an innovative philosophy with spirituality. Joseph Smith is without a doubt God's ultimate favorite demonsapien and possibly residing in the second Dimension of Demonic Existence. God is most pleased with the brilliant mind of Joseph Smith. No other demon since then has been nearly half as impressive. Unfortunately, a clan of jealous demons murdered him, but his legacy continues to live along with his teachings.

Other famous demons originating from out of the Western Culture and referred to as cult leaders are L. Ron Hubbard, Father Divine, Jim Jones, and David Koresh. All have come and gone to demonstrate the power of demonic influence but on a much smaller scale. None of them were nearly half as successful on a universal scale as Joseph Smith. His message has converted more than 130 million demons. Some demons like to believe that Joseph Smith will return and add a continuation to his personal revelation.

Demonsapiens also have attempted to impress God by committing a mass of human massacres either all at once or over a long period of time. The most notorious demon known to man is Adolf Hitler, who was responsible for the massacre and torture of more than 6 million demons within a time span of twelve years. There is yet another well-known demonsapien, representing the United States by the name of Timothy McVeigh. He bombed the Alfred P. Murrah Federal Building in 1995 and exterminated 168 demons, and injured another 680 all at one time.

Timothy McVeigh is the most disappointing and worst demon from the entire Western hemisphere for the reason that murdering another demonsapien is not impressive to God since we naturally are demonic. Demons committing demonic acts are no different from a dog doing tricks for treats. God does not smile upon the idea of human slaughtering, even though we have the free will to decide what to do with our bodies.

Those known for creating cults, new religions, and spiritual movements usually end up despised by other demons and a great abundance of spiritual warfare is destined to follow them. Subsequently, innovative demonsapiens are bound to fail against the larger scale of faiths that govern across the globe with prehistoric demonnations. It seems merely impossible to restructure the minds of living demonsapiens that follow the oldest beliefs. Revealed religions have already placed root in the mindset of dependent demons. Many have already committed to these beliefs by handing down its earliest teachings of religious sectarianism. It has taken more than an army of demonsapiens to maintain the dogma of an age-old belief like for example, Catholicism.

Wars have always been a demons second desired method to strategically entertain God but not half as brilliant as religion. However, looking at wars from a broader scope, or outside of the Western spectacle, you will find endless political demons fighting for God's attention.

The United States has had plenty of homegrown political war demons like George Washington, Abraham Lincoln, Woodrow (Thomas) Wilson, Franklin Delano Roosevelt, Harry S. Truman, Lyndon Baines Johnson, Richard Milhous Nixon, and Ronald Wilson Reagan. Crossing into other territories makes all of these demons by far the most impressive. Not one could have done it alone, as it had to take armies of demonsapiens to transpire multiple demonic casualties on foreign soil. Most of them have said that it was to protect the American people and in the name of God.

As demons reside on earth, there are two rules that need following. We do not have the right to destroy or cause harm on another demonsapien unless it is with their permission. Our body is a loan that we should care for or destroy. However, we should never do harm to another demon's body. In addition, there is also a part of the human body to treat with love and respect at all times. The most crucial rule is to respect and protect the human genitals. If we show ourselves worthy, we will protect our genitals so the sub-deity can reside there.

The greatest challenge for all demonsapiens is learning a new way of thinking in order to be content on earth. All demons have the gift of knowing what good is. Some will accomplish good deeds while others will develop positive relations.

Love is not one of the familiar qualities that demons were born with, if there is such a meaning. Realistically speaking, fewer demons in the world will know what love is let alone, will ever find it in another demon. Being kind to one's self and to others more so than anything else is the way to make an impression on God. Unfortunately, the great majority of demonsapiens are not willing to demonstrate a God-like quality of kindness and it is understandable.

"Live and let each demon live." This is the God-like quality to understand. It is not human nature but demonic nature.

Chapter 3
DIMENSIONS OF DEMONIC EXISTENCE

Within every belief comes a basic concept. According to True Cock Worship, all people are demons as well as being the primary basis to defining the characteristics of all human existence. There are Three Dimensions of Demonic Existence and Three Divinities of Demonic Evolution within Demonsapienism.

The Three Dimensions of Demonic Existence are the endless cycle of life, death, and life after death, which all demonsapiens will experience at some point. While in the first dimension, two very distinctive categories break down the life of

Demonsapienists. They can discover true intelligence or become a True Cock Worshiper.

The first Dimension of Demonic Existence is to reside on earth in the form of a human with the realization that we are all demons. Theoretically, Demonsapienists believe that the soul will depart from the body once dead. The soul completely passes through the first dimension in order to enter the second dimension, hence becoming an etūdame or etkić.

Etūdames and etkićs are dead demons that reside in the second Dimension of Demonic Existence. Their names originate from the founder of Demonsapienism to differentiate between two demonic entities that come from the second Dimension of Demonic Existence.

There is no place for the soul to wander in limbo, like purgatory, during the transition from demonsapien to etūdame or etkić. As demonsapiens pass through the plethora of radiance, we will recall wonderful memories and a series of events that happened when alive. Unfortunately, memories for the most part are recollected mostly during the transformation from demonsapien to etūdame or etkić. After the transition from one dimension of life to the next, the etūdame and etkić will have two dimensions for their entertainment. Demonsapiens have only one dimension to reside in. The most ironic part about being a demon is how the etūdame and the etkić are more alive than we are because they have the ability to enter our dimension as well.

Demonsapiens have the right to be atheists when there is little evidence or faith to believe in anything else. The only option an atheist has when residing in the second dimension is to exist as a molecule. They will be able to remember the past, see us, hear us, and feel us. Unfortunately, they will not have the ability to return the touch, be seen, or even heard by anything. Atheists will vanish practically into nothing of importance. They will become a part of the matter that surrounds us but not be harmed or punished for disbelief. The atheist will remain in this state for nine centuries and then released for demonic evolution and a new beginning.

While atheists morph into the matter that demonsapiens are surrounded by, Demonsapienists will pass into the second dimension with other options. Demonsapienists will have the option of re-experiencing life on earth in true form (looking as an etūdame or etkić) or dwelling into the midst of misplaced happiness (a place of bliss).

Demonsapienists believe that they can become enlightened by recognizing and acknowledging both dead and living demons. They also have the same amount of energy that both the etūdame and the etkić have. The only difference is that demonsapiens were born with fear. Fear is a choice and a demonic decision. God has no part with influencing this thought process. God is neither responsible for a demon's fears, decisions, or losses and should never be accused of one's misfortunes. After death, we will have a better understanding of our explanation for life and why fear exists and whatnot.

Demons residing in the first dimension do not know that they have the physical, mental and emotional capability to withstand demons from the second dimension. Whether it is an overwhelming amount of hatred or passion collected from the energy of an etūdame or etkić, it is often too much for the human body of a demon to handle.

When an etūdame haunts a demonsapien, the consequences are usually very traumatic and horrifying. Demonsapiens in the first dimension can fall victim to the personal interests of etūdames from the second dimension. This type of relationship is always a trap and never healthy for any demonsapien, however, it is necessary that we know what they want.

Demonsapiens need to avoid having encounters with etūdames because they are never present with good intentions. They will cause havoc on the living because they know that we are vulnerable to them. Dead spirits were never meant to intertwine with living spirits for any reason. These two dimensions will never be compatible with one another. This is why so many demons in our dimension have such negative lasting effects after an encounter with an etūdame. The conflict is always dead jealousy against living fear. There will never be a way to escape a relationship like this without experiencing some form of psychological trauma.

Demonsapiens that are accused of being controlled by a demonic possession should leave the accusers and seek psychiatric care with a non-biased professional. If the one being accused does not have the sound mind to rescue him or herself, the one who sees the problem should help deliver the victim from their environment, with proper authorities. Individuals that are accused of demonic possession are believed to be under emotional duress, with some form of mental illness or stressed by life itself.

Most demonsapiens have learned that demons are separate entities lurking about and waiting to enter a vulnerable human. Many have been raised to believe that a demon is an evil entity that seeks a host, or in other words, an individual to live in. They believe that these are lost souls unable to cross over into the next life. Since Demonsapienists believe that we are already demons, there is no such thing as a separate entity aside from ourselves. Exorcisms are only performed on dead demons also known as etūdames but never demonsapiens. Etūdames are not in limbo trying to cross over. They already have passed but through the second dimension. Dead demons return to the first dimension because they can. They need to be chased away or out from the place where they are disturbing the peace.

Demonsapienists do, however, believe that exorcisms should be performed under certain circumstances. Exorcisms are not condoned when there is clear visible evidence that an entity is present. Etūdames are identified primarily by sight, and they are not human looking in any way, shape or form. Some have the ability to speak a native tongue, but they are often known to giggle, snarl, growl, hiss, make clicking sounds and other strange noises. Etūdames should be confronted and dealt with by a Demonologist, a professional exorcist, or another demonsapien that does not fear them.

Individuals that do not have the ability to confront this kind of entity are encouraged to take whatever precautions they can by adopting a faith that knows what to do about it. Any denomination that knows how to destroy the relationship between the two dimensions is suitable. Demonsapiens that are in the company of an etūdame must have the entity removed by any means necessary.

Etūdames have the ability to cause permanent harm on the living and will do so by attacking, terrorizing, and revealing themselves in a natural state. They do this as a form of jealousy and revenge upon the living. The activity of an etūdame is nothing to fool with. We can know when they are present based on many clues. They do not have a problem making themselves visible in the daylight. An etūdame does not have shame in revealing their true ugliness. They in fact find it humorous that demonsapiens are easily terrified by seeing them this way.

Expect strange and/or supernatural occurrences when they are present. The signs are evident if you pay close attention. We can notice their presence based on drastic changes in room temperature, unnatural sounds, sudden changes in mood and other obvious signs. Many of them smell like gasoline, lighter fluid, smoke from a wood fire, or sulfur. Others might smell like the bad habit they once had when they were alive such as cigars, cigarettes, alcohol and narcotics.

We must study dead demons because they are our ancestors and our origin is identical to theirs. The only way to study them is to be aware of them and respect their presence. Please acknowledge the significance of the etūdames and the etkićs, as you will someday become one or the other.

Some of us have the ability to see the etūdame or etkić in true form, and this is a remarkable gift. You should call yourself very fortunate - or unfortunate - when an etkić or an etūdame feels the liberty to reveal its true self. However, you must know that the etūdame are not in our presence for good reasons like with the etkić. The etūdame are hard on us and have high expectations if they are kin. They will visit when we have said or done something that triggers their direct attention. Etūdames take very seriously their mission and have the authority to terrorize. Spiritual laziness is what brings these demons around because we cannot always see the value of being alive.

On the other hand, demonsapiens that become religious fanatics are more susceptible to demonic invitation. A demonsapien will easily become an etūdame's spiritual playground. When we do not have an interest to entertain God by bad deeds, they might view us as a pathetic waste to society. Etūdames look upon us as living waste in the eyes of God. We can therefore become fair game to the spirit world for harassment based on this very reason. They will reveal themselves in disturbing ways to get our attention, but they are not around to cause fear without a valid reason.

The etūdame do not always travel alone. In fact, these wandering demonic spirits have the ability to multiply quickly depending on the situation. The etūdame enjoy visiting demonsapiens regardless. They do not care about the good deeds of a demonsapien. In fact, good deeds are what make a living demon even more a target. The etūdame will show support for any kind of ugliness. They are also present when there is good because being good invites more evil.

The best way to earn respect is to face the etūdame alone and then correct your spiritual path by becoming a Demonsapienist or studying it. An etūdame might not go away until you stop and speak with God by addressing Shem with an apology followed by asking what is required of you. At that very moment, correct yourself before your maker and then apologize to the etūdame for not showing respect for your demonic lineage. You will receive much more respect from the spirit world by presenting a sincere demonic declaration of guilt and bravery.

Demonic entities can become our worst enemies, and this is a warning that all demonsapiens must understand. They can become our protectors if we believe in Demonsapienism. We can learn to adapt to them or fear their presence. We can take heed to the warnings or continue to offend. Demons can protect or harm us. If we respect the voice of reasoning that initially comes from God, they will not invade our space.

Unless we surrender our soul or are murdered through a spiritual battle, an etūdame cannot take possession over another demon. If you surrender your body to an etūdame, you will find yourself in the second Dimension of Demonic Existence beginning a new journey.

Many demonsapiens have the ability to direct negative energy towards other demonsapiens. Demonsapiens are able to transmit their negative energy without ever having to be present or in the same room. Just as an etūdame, he or she will begin spiritual warfare out of spitefulness and jealousy. More often than not, the negative energy that is invading the space of an innocent demonsapien is mistaken as an etūdame. Oftentimes it is another living spirit with a very negative and bad spirit. Since the negative energy is coming directly from a living demon, he cannot remain present in another demonsapien's space for long. Demonsapiens such as this will make other demonsapiens uncomfortable for as long as they can, leave and then return when their energy level of negativity is at its highest. These demonic individuals are indeed bad spirits that never hesitate at being themselves.

If you go into physical battle with another demonsapien, the one who loses life in the first dimension will become the superior survivor. The one who's life expires first will have the power in the second dimension to return for revenge, if fortunate enough to remember you.

Demonsapiens that have the ability to take their memories with them after passing through the light will and can return to haunt and abuse. We will also have the opportunity to return through one of the Three Dimensions of Demonic Evolution. Never underestimate an etūdame and never forget to respect or recognize the spirit world for what it is worth.

Encountering an etūdame does not always mean that they are direct kin. In fact, it is more common for etūdames to be a stranger in our presence because they are harder for us to identify. Etūdames are impatient, desperate demons. They will do anything to get God's attention. What they want should not be taken personally because they are desperate for the same new beginning that we have. Knowing what they want, from their point of view, is understanding the nature of the beast in both of us.

In the second dimension, we will be able to design our own series of events that will affect the living just as dead demon have. The etūdame and the etkić have had the ability to design supernatural events. This remarkable ability enables some of them to connect with loved ones. However, seeking a loved one in this dimension might be uncommon due to the obliterating memory process. In other words, whomever they once connected with in the first dimension will become irrelevant or long forgotten.

As we all know, life is a cycle. Eventually the opportunity to return to earth through a terrestrial journey and to explore a new way of life will come. When it is our time to return by a quintessence of flesh, such as a human, God will allow the same liberties as before. We also can return as an animal or through some form of nature. As demonic souls, we will forever seek rejuvenation and supernatural occurrences.

As we wait in the second dimension, the world as we know it will remain depressed by the endless cycle of demonic life and death experiences. However, demonsapiens from newer generations will want to know the truth and change the future. Religious conformity will flush down the toilet just as culture and traditions will greatly deplete and/or become grossly modified. History will be reinvented by the ingenuity of young minded demonsapiens who will want to embrace and explore true intelligence. Every time a demon is reborn, we will witness a new phase of this reality.

As the etūdame and etkić transform into their natural state of demonic ugliness, they will have the ability to return to earth on unique occasions, and with God's knowledge.

Only in the second Dimension of Demonic Existence will an etūdame or etkić be able to return as a ghost or other familiar oddities that affect the essential welfare of the living. It is not common for them to return with the same physical human identity however, it is not impossible.

Life is a cycle of demonic existence. Demonsapienists believe that they can become enlightened by recognizing and acknowledging both dead and living demons. The primary responsibility for any etūdame is to remain in the second dimension for the same amount of years that they resided on earth.

Etūdames are very intelligent because they have a better understanding of the world that does not make sense to us. They already have discovered that there is no place in the second dimension commonly known as hell. Etūdames cannot be damned for punishment no matter what they do. There is no telling how many times that we, too, have experienced this phase of demonic transition, but it is meant to be forgotten. The most remarkable form of reality is to finally accept both living and dead demons as one species.

Aside from etūdames acting out in their natural state of ugliness, there is also another kind of demon populated purely by good deeds. Some faiths refer to them as angels but Demonsapienists refer to them as etkić. The etkić are just as active and have all of the same rights and free will as etūdames. They choose to be personal saviors and will go to enormous lengths to change their demonic mannerisms in hopes of correcting their discernible, physical hideousness.

Although the etkić and etūdame are similar in appearance, personality is what makes them distinctively different. Every moment that an etkić resides in the second dimension is depressing because of their appearance, becoming the good for society is their solution to dealing with self-loathing for a speck of happiness.

These so-called angels believe they are doing work for the Lord so that God will allow them to have complete control over the demonic evolutionary phase. In other words, they hope God will honor their wishes for being good and not put them in an undesired transformation. It is their ultimate desire to return once again as an attractive human without completing a full chander (a completion of three lifetimes on earth). Sadly, this is only dreaming on their part. Nonetheless, the etkić are always pleasant spirits to have here.

The third Dimension of Demonic Existence is where one of the Three Divinities of Demonic Evolution takes place. It is the most crucial stage because fear is the uncertainty of facing a transition that might be less than ideal. Both the etūdame and the etkić are aware of this phase and make a point to prepare for their part in the decision making process.

Demons will have the option to choose from any of the Three Divinities of Demonic Evolution when entering the process of sexual reproduction. God already knows how we wish to return, so it is not open for discussion. Unfortunately, the third dimension is the most crucial for all because it is the only time we will not have the option to dictate our destiny.

Even after performing good deeds as so-called angels, we still could return to earth in a less than desirable state. This is the final stage, but it only affects those that have completed three chanders. For example, demonsapiens have the right to blame God for being born with a physical or mental abnormality but generally do not. We have the right to blame God for a disappointing transformation, but generally do not. We can try to negotiate our return through one of the Three Divinities of Demonic Evolution, but ultimately God becomes the decision maker of our blueprint. The new product that we will become is solely in God's hands.

Those who wish to return in human form must complete a lifecycle of all three dimensions. Three lifetimes makes one complete chander. Demonsapienists believe that everyone must complete at least three chanders (nine lifetimes) to return as a human. Individuals like Gandhi and Princess Diana have already completed at least three chanders before returning to demonstrate their appreciation for life.

Most demons never will reach the magnitude of expectancy that would allow them to alter their own destiny. Ninety-nine percent of demonsapiens will remain enslaved by laziness and permanently dependent on the God of this universe. Most will return to earth having to repeat the same cycle that God designed.

The benefit of dying as a True Cock Worshiper is beyond what anyone is able to fathom. They will not have to experience another chander because they will be in the process of establishing their own universe. If a True Cock Worshiper is able to give honor to God through loving someone else's genitals until death, they will run circles around 120 billion galaxies after death. They will create their own universe in the process. They will share a collection of harmonious wisdom with other True Cock Worshipers. An exchange of thoughts with other Gods before them will become dynamic. There will be peace within these universes. True Cock Worshipers will have no perception of time after death. Everything will become infinite as time will become irrelevant. They will become an abundance of light and full of life. Each universe will birth another, forming new dimensions of lineage and, literally, distant kin.

True Cock Worshipers will become the God of their own galaxy but not unless they find a recipient in the first dimension to care for until death. If a True Cock Worshiper remains with the same recipient until death, he or she will become the oxygen that all demons require for life. It is indeed a sacred and spiritual marriage but not literally by the laws of demons. If servants of God want to keep the same recipient, they must make a habit at performing all of the rituals that demonstrates their commitment to God. Oral commitment demonstrates how much servants are committed to God.

Recipients that are able to endure until the end have the same opportunities that a True Cock Worshiper will receive. They too will become the Lord of their own universe as long as they can remain honest and faithful to the practice. Recipients also must keep a sacred vow.

Both will have the power to begin and end another demon's life by their own liberty and within another God's galaxy. However, interfering with the life of another civilization is not a desire. The gods of other galaxies have a mutual respect for one another and do not abuse their power like this.

Astronomers believe in something called Lagrange points and use other terminology regarding this universe. Such terminology is only for this universe. Demonsapienists, however, believe in more than one universe and the possibilities of an infinite amount of unique constellations both above and below our own. They believe that other life existences reside on visible layers also known as other dimensions or a serial plane of universes.

While most demons believe in one ultimate God, Demonsapienists believe that there are other universes far more unimaginable with an ultimate God over every kingdom of every universe. Demonsapiens have only had the ability to travel this universe from one dimension. This is the only universe that demonsapiens have ever known and studied.

God is indescribable, especially if going back to the beginnings of time. For each universe, a God is present and is the head of all its creation. Each God came from a previous God, who also came from another God. The God of aliens bred the God of demonsapiens. The God of aliens is one of many Gods and believed to be without gender, whereas the God of this universe is intersexed. Demonsapienists refer to the God of this universe as Shem. There is no hierarchy among the Gods since all have the same privileges however, seniority comes through birthing and aging other universes.

Out of every universe before us, the only God we can know something about is the God of aliens. The God of aliens appears to be the most lackadaisical by allowing the liberty of its creation to explore everywhere without a passport. Aliens are free to seek and explore their lineage through extraterrestrial pilgrimages. Extraterrestrial travelling is a common courtesy among the Gods. Unfortunately, the only active travelers that we know of at this time are aliens. Aliens come from a completely different dimension and are able to enter whatever dimension they so choose, including two of ours.

Demonsapienists believe that aliens visit because they know we are distant kin to them. They are very fascinated by us but have a poor way of communicating this. Demonsapienists also believe that aliens are attracted to us because we look more like them when in a natural demonic state.

When living demons have personal encounters with aliens, it is usually because they are studying our genetic tissue for their own aesthetic appeal. They have the desire to look human just as we have the desire to physically travel beyond the moon.

Those who believe in extraterrestrial beings believe that aliens have a place within this universe, but Demonsapienists do not. In this universe, there are the etkić (dead demons that want to do right), the etūdame (dead demons that do whatever they want), demonsapiens (living demons), and atheists (believers of nothing but self).

True Cock Worshipers, also identified as Demonsapienists, prefer to be in a special category based on their belief and philosophy. They believe aliens have existed for more than 90 billion years and that there is plenty of life beyond what we can fathom, but we must die in order to experience this realization.

Presently, all of us reside in a world beyond our choice with similar sexual perversions just as the God who designed it. Unfortunately, most demons refuse to accept this belief due to a narrow mind. True Cock Worshipers want demonsapiens to accept their sexual desires because the God of this universe created us this way. All true servants believe that the most important part about being alive is fulfilling the ultimate commitment to God by the use of sex.

Chapter 4
DIVINITIES OF DEMONIC EVOLUTION

There are Three Divinities of Demonic Evolution and two levels of spirituality within Demonsapienism. The Divinities of Demonic Evolution is the process in which a demon decides how they will return to earth.

One of the Three Divinities of Demonic Evolution is to become human. Westerners still hold to the belief that there are but two genders. The male and female gender is our primary distinction in life and death because this is what we have learned. Demonsapienists, however, do not support this conclusion and believe that demons are genderless until identified in human

51

body form. This identity also includes a demon's transformation into a fetus.

Many demonsapiens are not content with what God arranged. However, we have the right to modify and claim whichever sex we prefer to be. This option is only feasible after the demonic evolution process is complete. Three complete chanders are required in order to return once again as a human.

After the process of demonic evolution is completed, a demon will have the option to embrace or dislike what God has made of them. The God of this universe is intersexed and indifferent regarding the sexes. Therefore, if a demon is not content with the way he or she was born, then they should change it. No one, not even a parent, should take away that right. There is no judgment by God or consequence for transforming the penis into a vagina because the spirit of the sub-deity would not be present with a demon in this particular state of mind.

The first level of spirituality is dealing and coping on earth as a demonsapien. The second level of spirituality is when both the etkić and etūdame are ready to choose from one of the Three Divinities of Demonic Evolution. They will be able to have an effect with nature by becoming a part of it. It is a gamble returning in the form of nature for a chance that an etkić or etūdame might return as a termite or anything imaginable. Both the etkić and etūdame are destined to affect certain parts of our environment in positive and/or negative ways.

Since the etkić and etūdame do not have a body to play in, they might choose the second Divinity of Demonic Evolution just to return in the body of an animal. It is also the second level of spirituality. Both the etkić and etūdame believe they will serve only a short period of time in the first dimension of demonic existence if they return as an animal. It is also their opportunity to attack and or kill as a form of revenge upon the living. The body of an animal is used in malicious ways to cause harm. Animal abuse is one of the many demonic sports and forms of abuse that the etkić and etūdame might have to go through just to re-experience being human on earth.

For example, demonsapiens in the first Dimension of Demonic Existence might create a dogfight. One dog is forced to battle another as a gruesome sport and end up harmed or dead in the process. It could be a very short or long hard life if an etūdame or an etkić chooses this route. Demons coming from the second dimension have a mission here on earth. They believe it is worth it, though. Returning as an animal can become high risk just to shorten a chander period. Their mission is selfish, but we must respect them regardless.

God is pleased and amused by all that he created but demonsapiens, also known as humans, appear to be his favorites. We are characterized by certain levels of demonic mentality, some more severe than others. All humans are demons but not created in God's own image. We are perfect creatures that simply cannot resist fiendish behaviors, in God's eyes. We are probably God's most intelligent species, but for the most part are unable to make sound decisions without some form of demonic leadership.

From a Demonsapienist's point of view, believing that all of us were born with sin is false. Being washed away of sins is not feasible because we are demons. We can go through a religious cleansing for so-called sins but it will never make us better individuals. There is no such thing as wrong when a demonsapien is not harming anyone but himself. Self-inflicted harm comes from demonsapiens that are not content and do not understand their origin, what they are, where they come from, and why they might want to harm other demonsapiens.

"So called" humans can continue to believe that God made us in "his" own image, but then we would have to start worshiping one another. We also can be the true demons that we are and make God into our own liking, just as so many have already done. According to Demonsapienism, God is in all things, but not all things are in the image of God. We are still Shem's favorite creation above all else.

The place where we as demons have failed most is in denying that God's true love and existence is through the human genitals. Human sexuality has always been the most precious gift that God can give us, but we are led to deny this through shame, embarrassment, guilt and alienation. It is more common to be led away from sexual inhibitions by other demons that want to hinder us. Most individuals do not believe that we can establish God-like qualities through the human genitals.

However, they can follow the teachings of any demonsapien they wish. They also can deny their own sexual revolution or respect the philosophy of Demonsapienism and explore it. Either way, the most attractive part about being alive is human sexuality.

Chapter 5
PHILOSOPHY OF TRUE COCK WORSHIP

True Cock Worship is an extended philosophy of Demonsapienism that exercises the elements of sexuality with spiritual overtones. You will never appreciate the philosophy of True Cock Worship if you are looking at human sexuality as ungodly and degrading outside of wedlock.

As with any belief, you must be able to find logic in all that it stands for in order to believe in it. What a demonsapien cannot understand usually becomes difficult to accept. It is essential to recognize and respect the spirit world for what it is worth.

Demonsapienists and True Cock Worshipers are able to recognize one another by a fair exchange of thoughts and ideas. They also have a lingo unlike anyone else and use the same glossary of words. Since True Cock Worship is a Western concept, various terminologies from other beliefs like Hinduism for example, is not applicable.

True Cock Worship eliminates shallowness and builds acceptance for all. It is a logical concept for individuals that know what they want sexually. True Cock Worship helps establish healthier interactions and brings improbable spirits together. It breaks down walls and barriers regarding the taboo world of sexuality, relationships and spirituality. It celebrates individuality, brings intimacy to individuals, and introduces a new perspective for those who have not yet discovered a compatible counterpart.

Some demonsapiens enjoy debating the concept of everything under the sun, including what is true regarding someone else's belief. There is nothing wrong with standing by what one believes, but no one has the right to force their belief on someone else. Disputing anything that appears sacrilegious is ignorant and narrow minded, therefore, arguing with, or going against a Demonsapienist is considered amusing. There is humor in being argumentative regarding what is not God. Having judgmental characteristics is typical of a demon. Servants of God simply believe that anyone that has a faith, be it good or bad, has a belief true to them. As we all know, there are a list of requirements that come within each belief. The list of requirements makes a demonsapien rightfully able to claim their faith.

True Cock Worshipers and Demonsapienists believe that God designed a perfect universe for all of his creation to use for entertainment and selfish pleasures. Both believe they have the free will to live without religious conformity and do not support anything that hinders them from happiness.

Religious conformity is also one's right and non-believers are entitled to their opinion. However, ideologies that come from other spiritual sectors that inaccurately interpret Demonsapienism, do not receive credibility. The teachings of

Demonsapienism can only come from a true Demonsapienist, a supportive counterpart for Demonsapienism.

While there are benefits in the life of a cock worshiper, it can become a dangerous lifestyle to practice. It is especially dangerous when an individual has not learned or accepted the philosophy about how to deal with demons. Anyone can suck on a penis, but they are not "true" to the spiritual essence and craft of true worship until they have embraced the concept of Demonsapienism.

Committing to the philosophy of Demonsapienism separates all True Cock Worshipers from other cock worshipers that are not "true" to the essence. Those that are not "true" are those that refuse to accept the fact that they too are demons. Demonsapienists do not have to be True Cock Worshipers, but it appears hypocritical not to be at least supportive of it. If you do not like performing or receiving oral sex, it will be impossible to live the life of a True Cock Worshiper.

Embracing the oral aspect with the presence of the sub-deity is a major obligation. Oral worship is a physical obligation that allows demonsapiens to have an intimate experience with God. There is no other option. You must love sucking on the penis or love having your penis sucked on in order to appreciate this faith.

While several elements exist in the mental state of a servant of God, the number one element is to be one with Shem through the human genitals. True Cock Worshipers often make a point to remember who their god is and why they pray, meditate upon, and worship the penis. They dedicate themselves to oral worship, but like anything else it is within logical reasoning and moderation. Servants of God do not like to perform oral sex without prayer and meditation first. It helps them to make good decisions and God is most pleased when they are able to find a suitable candidate.

True Cock Worshipers constantly face having to keep the right state of mind by disciplining themselves at maintaining a clear and separate distinction between the deman and his penis. This state of mind can be the most difficult since the greatest test for any servant is to remain consciously aware of these two differences. They must learn to manage a way of tuning out distractions that come from other demons during prayer and worship by the use of meditation.

The risk is higher for an inexperienced Demonsapienist that has blasphemed with disbelief in the past. They could risk being in a spiritual battle with an etūdame. For this reason, beginners should not meditate after sundown. Becoming a worshiper of the penis is one attribute that many demons in general claim to have already achieved without meditation and prayer. However, being able to develop peace and harmony with demons from the second dimension (without prayer and meditation) is a whole other skill and attribute.

Some demonsapiens have spent nearly their entire life acting as spiritual wanderers. Many have sought how to combine sex, prayer and worship without shame and guilt. Most individuals do not know how to let go of these psychological hindrances. Sexual burdens is liable to haunt anyone that is still holding on to religious traditions. A follower of God never goes punished for exploring his or her sexual desires. Shem waits for individuals not to fear the judgment of other demonsapiens.

True Cock Worshipers define true salvation as the moment when an individual is finally able to abandon their sexual hindrances. True salvation only comes after they have let go of the spiritual complexities and anxieties that have haunted them. It does not make sense to honor a God that requires us to be ignorant of our own physical and sexual embodiment. God does not punish for masturbating. Masturbation is a beautiful form of intimacy and a way for us to have a God-like experience.

True Cock Worshipers believe that God is not just for the sanctity of marriage because many demons never will marry. They believe that someday marriage will become obsolete. Money will not be wasted on this tradition. All demonsapiens will feel worthy of affection without judgment. The God of True Cock Worship does not place judgment upon individuals that take responsibility for their own sexual needs. It is also encouraged to find someone that will help fulfill these sexual desires. Once demonsapiens are able to accept that they are indeed demons, they will become open to receiving true salvation.

Demonsapienism is not the belief that humans are created in God's own image like the teachings of Christianity. True Cock Worshipers believe that God, the omnipotent, is whatever we so desire Shem to be. Shem will be, as long as Shem is, so Shem becomes. No demon with sound logic could possibly believe in a God without evidence, nor should they be forced to. If by faith we choose to believe in someone or something that cannot be seen, it is a personal right.

Unfortunately, like with any faith, Demonsapienists and True Cock Worshipers can fall away from their belief, and this is not a crime. Should a servant of God have a change of heart, there must be a goodbye ceremony. When a servant loses faith, changes belief, or no longer wants to be a Demonsapienist, they must present a burial. The servant must take everything used and burn it. This process purifies the spirit, erases the past, and allows a new beginning.

Servants usually invest in obtaining their own belongings for worship and rituals. They never sell or give away the items accumulated. True Cock Worshipers demonstrate their dedication to the faith by purchasing everything. Accepting a collection of items once used by a former True Cock Worshiper is bad luck.

Everything that belonged to the recipient is either burned or returned. Fire will destroy gowns, robes, books, manuals, photographs, illustrations and sculptures.

Once a servant has completed the burning ceremony, he or she then takes the ashes and puts it in a container large enough to dispose of. The last word a former True Cock Worshiper should say before walking away is "etū," which means, "that sums it up." Congratulations, you are now a Typical Cock Worshiper.

If you have claimed yourself to be a Demonsapienist with true intelligence, there is no ceremony. All you have to do is disclaim it by saying, "I am no longer a Demonsapienist." By

making this simple profession, it means that you do not believe
that all people are demons.

Chapter 6
PENIS, THE SUB-DEITY, AND DEMONIC WORSHIP

The Bible is right for teaching that it is not good for man to be alone only because the sub-deity, also known as the spirit of God, rests between the legs of Shem's creation. The penis is a counterpart to the omnipotent creator. Aside from the Vagina Goddess, the penis is the most precious part of all and is a holy place that is to be treated with praise at all times. True Cock Worshipers believe that God's peace, love and compassion come in the form of a penis. It is impossible for God to have wrath, jealousy or any negative connotation based on this concept.

The spirit of God knows that sexuality is the only language that demonsapiens understand. We can establish an ultimate closeness with God by spending time with the sub-deity. Servants believe that the Lord waits on individuals to discover Shem's spirit within the penis.

When it comes to religion, worship always has been a way to show respect for God. As far as universal beliefs, Judaism, Christianity and Islam all share much of the same history. We can find numerous passages within these three faiths that referred to individuals bowing their heads in worship. They would bow to thank the Lord for reasons that demonstrated their appreciation for a positive outcome.

While the Lord is depicted as a human with some religions, others are loaded with stories of individuals bowing down to worship a God they could not see. Most often, they would pray and worship their God through objects. Numerous stories have described how man worshiped images that represented God. The Torah and the Bible speak of images such as the golden calf, sun, moon, stars, works of their own hands, Daniel, Diana the Great Goddess, a golden image, angels, dragons, beasts, Satan, and Jesus. Neither the Torah nor the

Bible describes how man worshiped without the use of an object like the golden calf or the individual, Jesus.

Worshiping through the uses of objects is idolizing. Judaism, Christianity and Islam never actually provide a visible description of the Lord. Yet, all of these beliefs have a God with the ability to move, see, call, speak, make, set, create, bless, have, form, plant, grow, take, command, cause, know, walk, send, come, look, remember, enlarge, possess, deliver, give, talk, destroy, hear, open, tempt, tell, provide, endure, witness, meet, deal with, appear, go, cause, forbid, find, visit, hear and be jealous. A God having all of these so-called human characteristics, without actually being human, is difficult to fathom.

Questioning whether or not God has a body or a likeness to Shem is one of the many debates that religious scholars enjoy. They always have taught to have faith in something not seen, which explains why demonsapiens like to argue that the Lord does not need to be an illustration made real.

The book of Genesis mentions men having seen the face of God, but a description never was provided. The Torah and Bible cover numerous kinds of faces such as faces of men, faces of water, faces of the earth, as well as faces of nature. On the other hand, several individuals say reading a passage about God having a finger is not to be taken literally and is not any different from God having a body. Perhaps there is a misunderstanding about the body of God.

On the other hand, Demonsapienists recognize the omnipotent creator as tangible and within reach, when identified in the form of a penis. Some Demonsapienists believe that God is intersexed and becomes a masculine entity known as the penis as well as a feminine entity known as the vagina. They believe that no one can appreciate anything living without first acknowledging that everything living is a fragment of the Lord's existence. If an individual is not a True Cock Worshiper, God might only be obtainable by demonic pollution or true intelligence.

Some demonnations emphasize the oneness of God and believe that Jesus is God manifested in the flesh. They forbid you to wear a cross as some call it idolizing. Islam is just as unforgiving about presenting depictions of anything along the aspects of idolizing. Other religions have their own understanding about God. If more than one is illustrated it falls under the concept of polytheism. Whether or not an individual is monotheist or polytheist, most want to believe in something by faith or by sight.

True Cock Worshipers believe some penises have a spirit called the sub-deity. Unfortunately, this spirit is not present with all penises. Not all individuals will want to acknowledge the spirit of the Lord in this way. In fact, many will not, which is why God's spirit is only present with those that have respect for Shem in this form. The sub-deity is simply an extension of God, the omnipotent, but physically powerless. Shem is manifested in the form of a penis, patiently resting between the legs of eligible demans, that receive blessings with a servant of God.

It is important not to confuse True Cock Worship with Hinduism. The sub-deity is not defined as Lingam, phallus or penis. The penis itself according to True Cock Worship is the body of God and a separate counterpart. A penis without the sub-deity is the same as a corpse without a soul. However, with or without the sub-deity, have respect for the penis by referring to him as a lesser god, Lord, or Great Penis.

Just as Christianity has the trinity, True Cock Worship has what is called the quadruality. The quadruality are four distinctive parts consisting of the sub-deity (the spirit of God), the human genitals (the body of God), and the voice of reasoning (the logical consciousness of God that enables us to make good sound decisions). All are separate functions that become extensions of God. Not one is able to operate alone because God, the fourth concept, must be present. God is first a concept, secondly made into spirit called, the sub-deity.

The human genitals is the place where the Lord directly receives love from all creation. The voice of reasoning that directs the sound judgments of individuals comes not from any other but God. Each part of the quadruality operates in ways that can improve the nature of each individual. Not every demonsapien will utilize every part of God, but it is feasible.

When a demonsapien takes the initiative at obtaining the life of godliness, the voice or reasoning becomes the relationship that directs right from wrong. The voice of reasoning is simply a logical decision. Unfortunately, not all demons have the ability to listen to their voice of reasoning in fact, many do not. This does not necessarily mean that demons cannot hear the voice; they can but often ignore it.

Being able to identify the sub-deity helps servants to know when it is safe for them to use a particular individual for oral practices. The sub-deity only will reside with those that have the right frame of mind and utilize their voice of reasoning rather than acting on natural demonic impulses. We cannot have the right frame of mind without the guidance of our maker. The only way a demonsapien can experience the spirit of God is by adhering to the voice of reason.

Dead demons have the ability to corrupt our decision-making but they are in no way in control of the voice of reasoning. We cannot blame them or anyone for our wrongdoing. The right frame of mind allows a deman (male demon), to receive blessings through the sub-deity. The sub-deity has the ability to cause two or more individuals to come together for a good cause. The sub-deity has the ability to remember the affection it received from an individual and deliver nothing but positive energy.

Demans that are suffering from depression have no acknowledgment for the sub-deity that has the ability to hear their cry. They should know that happiness, peace, lust (love), stability, and rewarding friendships all come with the presence of the sub-deity.

Finally, yet most importantly, the penis becomes a part of the quadruality. It becomes the ultimate God manifested in the flesh. True Cock Worshipers base their faith upon a God that can be seen and has a body.

A deman can become financially successful based on his penis. It is common for a demonica (female demon), to seek out a deman based on the size of his penis. Great financial success comes to demans that treat their penis with respect. The penis can rise to leadership if given the opportunity. He can take orders but also has the ability to lead. The penis can set an example of how to be humble yet strong.

Not only can he come to any given occasion for a good cause, but he can also look at anything with optimism. He has the ability to enlarge with excitement and joy and possess anyone who adores him. The penis can tempt an individual into falling in lust as well as send off positive messages to anyone he chooses.

It is believed that the passage to life is procreation with the mindset to evolve. The sperm from a penis can produce life. The penis penetrates. Pierced is an egg. The penis sanctifies a demonica with the seed to bare a demon child. He has the ability to appear in every loving moment and remain humble when the attention is not on him. The penis can go with his vessel keeper on long journeys and is always with him. He will visit, if he is meet half way and can cause a release of tension. If the penis is well treated and nurtured in a loving way, the best of happiness will come to its vessel keeper. Furthermore, if a deman is willing to pray to his penis, he can be made worthy enough to create his own universe.

The penis can endure all types of pain and torture although he prefers not to. He can witness and feel a terrible break up, the loss of a loved one, and the terrible effects of substance abuse. The Great Penis presents all goodness and purity as well as hears a deman's sorrows. He can accept life with an open mind and deal with problems head on if properly acknowledged.

The sub-deity is powerless in physicality. Not all vessel keepers will obtain the embodiment of the Lord's presence between their legs. If this were the case, God would protect Shemself from most vessel keepers.

Demans with unacceptable traits can be accurately revealed with prayer and meditation. Once this determination is made clear, servants of God are absolutely forbidden to remain entertained by these kinds of demans. True Cock Worshipers should never waste their time with demans that foolishly disregard the worth of their penis. This does not mean that the deman does not have the potential to change; in fact, he can change with a lot of support and determination.

However, if the deman continues to think or speak in an unacceptable manor in regards to his penis, he is damning the rest of his life to loneliness. Demans that are mentally ill and constantly insult their penis are forgiven but only for a very short period. It is best to have mercy for the individual that shows obvious signs of mental illness by offering spiritual support. Those blessed with the sub-deity between their legs will forever appreciate a True Cock Worshiper's good deeds.

All of us can learn with an open mind how to connect with our deepest desires by worshiping God's existence through human sexuality. There are actual individuals in the world that go beyond the delight of playing with the lesser God. They will by praying to and meditating on Shem as a critical part in their daily life. Those who truly worship the penis will glorify, idolize, sanctify, love, praise, exalt, and bow down to Shem for prayer and worship.

Chapter 7
DO NOT WORSHIP MAN

The mind of a man is not impressive if he has to admit to his mistakes. He would much rather excuse his actions by blaming a part of himself that has no intellectual ability to do anything more than bring blessings and pleasure. Constantly blamed for recklessness is a man's penis. There is nothing more disgusting than a servant of God witnessing a vessel keeper insult his penis or speak less of his penis in this way. Men that fail at connecting with their penis on a spiritual level have a worthless mentality.

Most Westerners have never fathomed the idea of worshiping a penis let alone seen the benefit in it. Men always have displayed their emotions towards their penis by exhibiting complete supremacy over it. It is more common to believe the penis is nothing more than a tool, and this is very unfortunate. Life can become a personal obstacle for any vessel keeper who chooses to think this way. They are quick to blame their penis for any wrongdoing rather than apologize for being inadvertently responsible.

Most men do not notice the challenges faced by the greatness of their penis. They are unaware of the energy and great power that rests between their legs. The penis is the dominator and creator of all things. Men have both good and bad sides to them, but they are nothing more than demonsapiens that cannot help the true nature of their origin.

Most vessel keepers view the penis as but an object, but True Cock Worshipers believe that a penis beholds a powerful entity. It is very unfortunate that man is unable to manage his mind. He has been at war his whole life with his penis. All men have certain levels of passion. They will give until they have nothing left or will quickly rob your soul of everything. Men will buy themselves into anything as long as it benefits them because their desire comes first.

The mentality of a man is permanently disappointing. Almost all of them were born with egotistical characteristics. All were born naturally malevolent, and they will turn against you without remorse. They will forever inflict heartache because they cannot help but be shallow. Men can abandon not only their own spirit but also everything that has a spirit. All of them were born callous because they are demons.

Men have different characteristics in general, but most of them have the tendency to wander and speak about nothing of importance. It is a sad sight watching a man wander himself into a trench while pursuing selfishness and greed. They do not always know what they are saying or what they are doing. They will often exhibit actions and emotions that are difficult to comprehend. Most importantly, men never know for sure what they want. All of them are liars and each must be tested mentally, emotionally and spiritually to be made worthy of semi-cock or True Cock Worship.

Servants of God believe that man invented religion to deliver himself from his own sexual desires. He is responsible for teaching that it is shameful to lust and discovered a way to hinder himself from lusting after the weaker demons. Ethnicity, nationality and gender all fall under various kinds of weaker demons. Man also created a way to dominate the actions and behaviors of weaker demons by the use of physical and psychological abuse. It is therefore most essential to have first a spiritual and physical connection with a man's penis, since most of them lack character appeal.

Satisfying one's own sexual desires is not sinful as many claim God said. Man himself made up this assumption. His dominant and proud ego is undoubtedly responsible for every poisonous philosophy. God is not responsible for the books that man wrote and marked inspired by God. Having sexual restraint or sexual temptation is not from the Lord.

Most religions portray God as hateful and intolerant to place fear. Men of God will use their own so-called "expert judgments" against other men rather than come to accept their own ugliness. They might come across the teachings of Demonsapienism and say that it is wrong in the eyes of God. Do not worship or listen to these men because they have not found their own true intelligence.

True Cock Worshipers must remain cautious by knowing how to deal with each man under the guidance of Demonsapienism. They can know through prayer; as the spirit of God will tell them when they have met a man that is right for oral worship. Unfortunately, vessel keepers are mentally unstable and do not understand how being useful accommodates another demon's blessings. Men might not be the mental bearer of sexual energy but they are definitely the carriers of the physical. They have the ability to give the best part of themselves for the good of a servant's blessings.

Sadly, there is no cure for the mind of any man, according to Demonsapienism. True Cock Worshipers have learned to spiritually adapt to this unfortunate reality. It is pertinent that a servant of God remain dedicated to prayer for their mental state and for the reason that each man encountered is completely useless without his penis. Men are generally a waste of God's good air, but a servant cannot live without them because they are bearers of the holiest temple. Aside from the Vagina Goddess, all that is between the legs of a man is the holiest and the most sacred place on earth. If you have a penis, you carry the seed to true salvation and sexual enlightenment.

Chapter 8
COCKWORSHIPER

During the last fifteen years, the term "cock worship" has surged into a fast growing movement. Cock worshiping is a sexual act for which two or more individuals come together to experience sexual gratification. Westerners generally like to describe the act for oral sex as worship but there are other kinds of sexual worship. Cock worshiping is basically generalized, but there are two primary types of cock worship that can be referred to as typical or true. They are also divided into subdivisions that specifically aim at fulfilling the needs of individuals, sexually and/or emotionally.

The universal kind of cock worshiper is the Typical Cock Worshiper. What makes these individuals unique is their willingness to sacrifice their own dignity to satisfy a stranger. They will allow a deman to utilize his penis as a weapon that is most gratifying to himself. He will use his penis to face fuck, grudge fuck, rape, cock slap, and/or sodomize his cock-worshiping victim. The number of Typical Cock Worshipers around the world is unknown, however the age of these individuals appears to be getting younger. Typical Cock Worshipers are not hard to find. They can be found anywhere in the world. If a vessel keeper appears intriguing enough, a cock worshiper often will approach first.

Typical Cock Worshipers are always accessible and can be located at bus stops, parks, nightclubs, college campuses, wedding banquets, business expos, conventions, and even religious organizations. They are rated anywhere from classy to complimentary whores seeking intimate connections. Many of them are willing to perform oral sex without ever knowing a name. They are also more inclined to swallow the sperm of a stranger at the value of nothing, but there is a certain level of shame that follows. Interestingly enough, Typical Cock Worshipers do have a guilty conscious; perhaps it is religious conviction that haunts them. It is possible to find indications of a religious past through an underlying amount of unspoken indignity.

Religions often teach that sex outside of marriage is forbidden and people must be married to have this intimate right. Efforts to capture the interest of a Typical Cock Worshiper might be overshadowed by his or her own sense of guilt. There will always be a sense of guilt when coming from a religious background, and this explains why you might not ever see them again.

Typical Cock Worshipers are not prostitutes, therefore a price is not negotiated in exchange for a good time. They are simply easy demans and demonicas that are dedicated to the craft. There is nothing wrong with being typical in fact; Typical Cock Worshipers are some of the most beautifully spirited individuals on earth. It is a privilege to be in the presence of a Typical Cock

Worshiper. They are rightfully deserving of generous gifts from strangers due to their sexually good deeds. You can buy drinks, take them out to dinner, take them to see a movie, invite them to see a show, or even take them on a trip. There is no harm in presenting a Typical Cock Worshiper with a generous donation, but nothing is more satisfying than sexual reciprocation.

Typical Cock Worshipers also have a subdivision referred to as Cock Extremists and Cock Moderates. Whether a worshiper is extreme or moderate, all want to be at the complete mercy of a dominant deman. Both have a desire to please the dominant receiver in any way they can.

Typical Cock Extremists are the most intense and best known for their outstanding performance of emotional resilience. They are victoriously deranged by receiving repulsive humiliation with all types of high sexual risks. They will stop at nothing for brutal penile punishment. They are also confident about their claims at providing cock worship through great oral sex, amongst other things.

Some professionals would interpret the behavior of a Typical Cock Extremist as self-destructive and addicting. They repeatedly will submit themselves to sacrificial torment as if to tell Jesus that they are much better at being a victim than him. Many of them are known to have a damaged past, which makes falling in love or accepting sincere affection from another demon very difficult. Typical Cock Extremists are very passionate individuals. Unfortunately, they might have difficulty verbalizing their emotions and prefer expressing what they feel through actions.

There is also a deep level of mysticism within a Typical Cock Extremist's state of mind. They will appear as though they are seeking to be spiritually connected to something. Typical Cock Extremists might pursue a sadomasochist individual to cope with a damaged past. Some Cock Extremists will seek what is referred to as irrumation. It is when unknown individuals try to suffocate a Cock Extremist with their penis by forcing it down their throat until they vomit. Cock Extremists also will drink the urine of several strangers. It takes a lot of courage to be at the mercy of a complete stranger, which is why they are referred to as

Typical Cock Extremists, but these humiliatrix victims do have a demonic name.

There is no happy place for the mind and body of a Typical Cock Extremist to rest. It is quite common that they be slightly obese due to oral fixation. Many of them have low self-esteem and look to food as comfort. Caressing emptiness and the lack of companionship by overeating is not the best solution. It barely fills the void of insignificance from a damaged past. Some of them are the exact opposite of obese. Anorexia and bulimia is also a common illness among Typical Cock Extremist that hate themselves. They can become desperate enough to engage in committing dehumanizing acts with narcissistic individuals just for an opportunity to be recognized.

Typical Cock Extremist become further damaged as the list to escape from emotional suffering increases. Sexual recklessness easily defeats a Typical Cock Extremist. They are always trying to re-generate piety for their empty soul and it is a losing battle. They will never admit to idolizing other demonsapiens. The life of a Typical Cock Extremist is very distressing and lonely. They wish to receive a morbid form of compassion with a sadomasochist.

Dominant demans will seek out Typical Cock Worshipers for their commitment in performing oral sex acts as well as other things. They might be inclined to engage in situations with reciprocity; performing sexual acts for something in return. It is acceptable for Typical Cock Worshipers to take the liberty of engaging with several sex partners because they experience constant abandonment.

Not only is there a depressing aspect of being typical, but there is also an optimistic side to a Typical Cock Worshiper. Typical Cock Moderates redeem this title is by acting as slaves but not necessarily with strangers. The ability to satisfy through pure submission is a sensual endeavor that all typicals seek to accomplish.

Typical Cock Moderates have their limits. They are much more selective about their choice of demans and who will have permission to enslave them with a cock. Typical Cock Moderates enjoy manipulating a penis between every orifice and crevice they have. They will take the cock and put it between their breasts, buttocks, armpits, hands, feet and mouth as well as swallow sperm. Typical Cock Moderates might not want to admit it, but they carry many of the same exact psychological patterns of torment as their depressing twin, the Typical Cock Extremist. There is no doubt both types would try to make love with Satan himself if there was such an entity. As with all Typical Cock Worshipers, submissiveness is a choice that one makes by surrendering all rights over to one or more random individual.

There is also a small, but fast growing, subculture of individuals that call themselves True Cock Worshipers. True Cock Worshipers are only worthy of having this title by living under three distinctive principles. First, they are primarily Demonsapienists and proclaim the penis to be a living manifestation of God. Secondly, they look to the penis to discover the sub-deity, a spiritual element of True Cock Worship. Third, they live a life consisting of three spiritual obligations. Without these obligations, they are just Typical Cock Worshipers. Oral practice might be important, but it is not on the top list of obligations. It is impossible to be true to the faith without prayer and meditation as well.

Worship is literal in every sense of the meaning. True Cock Worshipers worship the sub-deity, the spirit of God, not the penis. Not every penis deserves oral worship, and oral worship is not foreplay. True Cock Worshipers begin and end with oral. Nothing else follows the act of oral unless a lover is used as a recipient.

Recipients can pass out or fall asleep only to wake up with the servant still between the legs in worship. If he ejaculates three minutes into the session, he will have to tolerate the rest of his time in a flaccid state because he is irrelevant. However long it takes to complete a True Cock Worshiper's session, the recipient must remain respectfully silent.

Irrumation is not one of the techniques that occurs during a worship session because typically it is an act of a dominant deman's control. Irrumation never will happen unless a True Cock Worshiper allows their spiritual guard down. Dominant demans always will run into a wall with a True Cock

Worshiper unless a servant is willing to surrender. Dominant vessel keepers never will be far above a Demonsapienist during a True Cock Worship session, but they sure will try.

Servants of God are known to be the most dominant of all cock worshipers. Their strength comes from the spiritual practices of Demonsapienism. They exude a unique energy and confidence when they are spiritually at their strongest. True Cock Worshipers are both spiritual and sexual demons by nature and often use the philosophy of Demonsapienism to attract the weak. They have two sexual traits. They are either completely dominant or have the ability to switch on and off from dominant to submissive. A servant is never purely submissive unless their lover manipulates them by the use of charm. Even then, good luck with that because it only lasts for a short period.

Dominant demans are used for semi-cock worship but with strong precautions. Prayer and meditation is most crucial when a dominant vessel keeper is about to volunteer and receive oral worship. Both will struggle for power but only one will succeed. A True Cock Worshiper is able to come out of a meditative state or partial meditative state before walking into a situation for semi-cock worship. By doing this, he or she can dominate the most aggressive vessel keepers. Aggressive demans are usually confused by this twist of fate. They seldom win against the servant that both prays and meditates.

With all that said, True Cock Worshipers suffer a great deal of misery but far less often than a Typical Cock Worshiper. True Cock Worshipers also live a vivid series of abandonment. The only difference between the two is that servants have learned to adapt and cope with abandonment through the belief in Demonsapienism.

True Cock Worshipers pray to cope with emotional anxieties, confusion, stress, anger and restlessness and sometimes it is due to lack of sex. Prayer is a way for servants to nurture their own mental and physical inadequacies as well as demonstrate their commitment to God. Ultimately, prayer is a strategy that helps them to engage with different kinds of demonsapiens on a daily basis.

The psychological nurturing of sexual inadequateness within American society appears to be non-existent. True Cock Worshipers dedicate their lives to changing this. Efforts to remain cordial with all demons is crucial. Preventable measures are taken to avoid burning a bridge that someday might have to be crossed again. Servants of God have a difficult time accepting bitter endings after a friendly encounter because the more bridges they burn, the less valued and desired they become to society. Burning a bridge is discouraged, but it is often necessary if a vessel keeper mocks his penis. His destiny will be damned to future loneliness.

One of the many great challenges that all True Cock Worshipers deal with is becoming vulnerable and forgetting whom to worship. The servant must be spiritually prepared before every new encounter and not rush an experience. Taking the time to pray will minimize the need for several volunteers. When there is no comfort through prayer, it might be a sign that a possible power struggle with another demon is ahead. It is crucial that a True Cock Worshiper never lose sight of the spiritual side and remains in the best interest of the sub-deity.

Each new demonic interaction is recognized and dealt with through random short silent prayers. True Cock Worshipers also pray to the sub-deity for many of the same reasons that some religions and other cultures do. They pray to the penis in hopes to have a fruitful life, an ideal spouse, successful fertility, and to celebrate a successful birth.

Lastly, True Cock Worshipers pray for and counsel individuals that feel inadequate about their penis. They are carefully selected because some have a very low self-esteem and psychological insecurities.

Individuals that feel inadequate about their penis can receive mercy from servants that believe they have a calling to nurture the psychological hindrances of these individuals. They believe that there is an important responsibility in society to care for them. These distressed souls are able to gain mental strength and emotional security from True Cock Worshipers.

Some recipients and volunteers have called True Cock Worshipers "goddesses." Society knows these goddesses best for consulting with individuals that believe they are sexually inadequate. Recipients have also described them to be trouble-free companions and ideal spouses. Referring to a True Cock Worshiper as a goddess is an extreme compliment, but they make a point to remain humble and not become self-righteous. They are not goddesses.

Trying to locate a True Cock Worshiper is not easy since they are very rare and difficult to identify. They generally live a private and secretive life. In most cases, you will never know that you have encountered one. They will not openly talk about their faith with strangers. The spiritual reasons behind oral worship is highly misunderstood and more trouble to explain than it is worth. True Cock Worshipers are aware that they could be sought out primarily for oral. For that reason, the teachings of Demonsapienism is instilled, and stressed that all demons have ulterior motives.

True Cock Worshipers might openly share their spirituality once comfortable enough. They do enjoy discussing sex and religion as one topic. If you have indeed become acquainted with a servant of God, then you can call yourself fortunate, but always respect their spiritual point of view.

All True Cock Worshipers have the liberty to practice their personal beliefs while acting as a member of a religious organization. They might take the liberty to sit and fellowship among an organization while believing in the Demonsapienism philosophy. Nothing discourages them from socializing with and visiting other demonnations; in fact, it is encouraged. However, most servants prefer not to fellowship because it makes their lives less complicated. Religious conformity is a difficult lifestyle for them to embrace.

If True Cock Worshipers do decide to fellowship, they would most likely adopt the Hinduism belief over everything else. The Hindu belief system appears most logical and has a god called Lingam. Some will want to combine Hinduism from the East with True Cock Worship from the West, but it can be very confusing.

There is a great responsibility for all regarding oral worship. Recipients can face a great burden when used for True

Cock Worship because their penis is a True Cock Worshiper's primary source for all blessings and praises. True Cock Worshipers are very selective about choosing an eligible deman for spiritual cock worship. Vessel keepers will always be subject to the prey of a servant that listens and watches their mannerisms. They are always looking to see what deman meets the necessary requirements. Most demans are unaware that they are being observed nor do they know exactly what those requirements are. Eligible volunteers or recipients should know that they are not randomly chosen but carefully handpicked and solely according to their good characteristics.

If you already know a True Cock Worshiper but still have not been chosen for semi-cock worship or True Cock Worship, understand that you too are being watched like a hawk.

A servant's number one obligation is to never forget whom to worship by keeping a vow with certain limitations. Both recipients and servants are encouraged to have a significant other or be in an relationship. They can have a lover and several volunteers, but once there is an eligible recipient, all volunteers must go accept for the lover. It is forbidden to have a lover, a volunteer, and a recipient all at the same time. If the servant does not have a lover, then he or she might have an unlimited amount of volunteers.

There is no limit as to how many volunteers a servant can have but it is to their discretion. In all cases, volunteers are easily replaceable unless a serious relationship develops. Both volunteers and recipients can become a lover but most often this does not happen due to not having the ability to establish a spiritual chemistry with the servant.

Aside from the oral aspects of worship, something miraculous happens when two sub-deities are present with two eligible demans. The way to know when two sub-deities are present is when two homosexuals are True Cock Worshipers. These kind of vessel keepers can instantly call themselves True Cock Worshipers when both have a deep spiritual connection to their own penis. The level of ecstasy is beyond comparison to any heterosexual experience. The fact that two penises are present is enough reason to have a divine experience. Both servants have the natural ability to accommodate not just orally but also by the use of each other's penis. They have twice as many ways to honor the sub-deity, more so than any True Cock Worshiping demonica does.

When two sub-deities are present, both servants can initiate docking and anything else that falls within respect of the sub-deity. True Cock Worshipers already know that they can never allow injury or permanent penile damage during a worship session. Urethral sounding is only permitted if the decision is mutual and the spirit of the sub-deity is with both servants.

Homosexuals have something very special that demonicas will never able to compete with. They can establish a unique relationship with another's penis just as they have with their own. Worship sessions can be reached to an unimaginable magnitude of ecstasy. Nothing under the sun can compete with two sub-deities because it is the most powerful kind of True Cock Worship. Sessions where two servants can become one with God is always sacred.

When two sub-deities are present but only one is a True Cock Worshiper, the focus must remain purely spiritual and dedicated to semi-cock worship. True Cock Worshipers that engage with vessel keepers that do not share the same spiritual views must prepare to meet with volunteers just the same as True Cock Worshiping demonicas. Whether a True Cock Worshiper is heterosexual or homosexual, he must make a point to pray before each worship session.

A homosexual or bisexual servant of God is four to seven times more likely to encounter demonic conflicts with other demans. True Cock Worshiping demonicas have the same dilemma. One penis is never enough and that is why prayer and meditation has to become a necessary strategy. Each encounter is always a risk. If a True Cock Worshiper overlooks or neglects his purpose, he might find himself clashing with a deman that has different motives.

Sounding the Great Penis is the only act that is not recommended in a semi-cock worship session. It is a very intense practice that is not appealing to every vessel keeper. A True Cock

Worshiper can sound himself but on his own time or after the worship session is over. A volunteer can assist the servant with sounding but only after the needs of the sub-deity have been met. If it is requested, a servant can sound his volunteer after semi-cock worship.

Both volunteers and recipients adore True Cock Worshipers because their ideas do not match what oral experts in general teach. Cock worshipers generally share many, if not all, the same techniques. Most oral experts do not emphasis the spiritual aspect of oral sex. They are primarily focused on addressing ways to service without providing what frame of mind to be in. They teach that falletio should be used as a strategy or an introduction for intercourse.

One individual is responsible for initiating oral (also known as foreplay) in hopes that it might lead to similar reciprocity. Many oral experts say that good oral experiences should be done with someone he or she loves or has a strong attraction to. They will often waste time by going into details about creating a nice physical setting that sets the mood for sex.

Some will go as far as to describe how fluffy the pillows or how dim the lights should be. True Cock Worshipers on the other hand are completely opposite of oral experts and do not want to be categorized with them.

There is very little a servant can do, other than to pray and meditate, when they do not have a recipient or volunteer to exercise the physical aspects of worship. Worshiping the penis sometimes helps to release small bits of endorphins with the taste of pre-cum. It is practically a matter of life or death for a True Cock Worshiper to taste pre-cum. If a servant of God cannot feed their desire to worship, eventually they will revert to the act of masturbating or just becoming a Typical Cock Worshiper.

Aside from prayer, masturbation is an act performed simply by using the power of the mind. True Cock Worshipers that know how to meditate the TCW way, will masturbate without touching their genitals. This remarkable ability demonstrates a personal achievement to meditate. Vaginal or anal insertion with the use of objects might become the result for those that do not know how to meditate.

If a True Cock Worshiper does not pray or meditate, they might not ever develop a committed relationship with God. They can easily go astray out of discouragement but always can get back on track with prayer and meditation. When a servant is at their strongest spiritually, a vessel keeper's feelings is always a last resort. He can be used for all he is worth, and then discarded without ever knowing why.

Servants of God realize that there will always be an unlimited amount of demans available. However, finding a volunteer that will change for the good of worship is merely impossible. True Cock Worshipers are rare, but recipients are just as rare.

Chapter 9
YOUNG DEMONS AND MASTURBATION

Most religions discourage the right to explore one's own body. Westerners generally will believe in anything written in the so-called name of God, according to their faith. Most such faiths hinder their sexuality and believe that sexual exploration (outside of wedlock) is detrimental to one's personal salvation. Masturbation, whether explored alone or with someone else, always has been forbidden.

The American culture forbids young demons from learning about their bodies. They are humiliated, disciplined, and/or punished for touching themselves. Americans in general believe that sex is impure, filthy and not to be discussed openly.

This pathetic mentality is handed down from generation to generation.

Unfortunately, by the time a demon child becomes an adult, it is too late. They have ignorantly matured by the time they are old enough to vote. It is most common for American wee to have a poor example for a parent. Most come from a broken home where breeding out of wedlock and lust is a prime example. Demon children often discover sex by exploring it in the company of friends and keep it a secret.

Sexual judgment is passed on even into adulthood. It is taught that sex should only be learned as an adult, both independently and discretely. Judgment and sexual shame continues to be handed down because these are the beliefs of North American morality. It is obvious that Americans do not care enough about the welfare of their offspring to teach them about their own body. Those that choose not to educate their own about human sexuality deserve to accept the consequences by raising the next offspring in poverty.

Although American youth might learn religion, morals, and values regarding sexual conduct, North American statistics do not demonstrate that these inherited teachings are working. Teaching young demonsapiens not to explore sex out of wedlock has led the United States into a disastrous youth breeding epidemic. Very few of them actually take the time to reflect on the morals and teachings, if any, that they were raised on. Their actions have spoken by acts of rebellion. There is no way to prevent young demonsapiens from breeding more unwanted demonsapiens. Promiscuity will continue to become a problem until the right role models personally teach their youth about human sexuality. They will continue to find out about sex on their own.

Americans have inherited this mental disease that has passed on for generations. They have no one to blame but themselves for having so much sexual narrow mindedness. Ultimately, the positive elements of sexual nurturing remains unexercised and uncelebrated because demonsapiens have deprived themselves and their own offspring of sexual liberation.

Other parts of the world are far more open minded about sexual exploration. Unfortunately, they have many obstacles to face within their laws. There is a universal mark of shame in the minds of many, but this is due to extended religious conformity and ignorance.

While American demonsapiens have a constitution that allows sexual exploration within law and reason, most choose to abide by the restrictions that come from inherited beliefs and traditions. Each generation continues to pass on the same pathetic explanation for damning what God created. Religion planted this mental corruption.

Understanding the purpose for human genitals is a must. Most individuals do not want to accept the fact that God created them for more than procreation and personal enjoyment. True Cock Worshipers believe that there is a spiritual reason why demonsapiens have genitals. Humanity should not remain ignorant about the purpose of human genitals because God designed them for giving and receiving blessings.

Masturbation is a godly attribute. Those that masturbate will show their appreciation to God for having genitals. Those that do not honor God in this way should abandon all other forms of happiness. Anyone who teaches that it is wrong to masturbate is an enemy of the creator. True Cock Worshipers believe that celebrating the human genitals is so sacred that anyone who feels guilty about doing it should not have arms.

Chapter 10
ORAL WORSHIP

One of the benefits to being known as a True Cock Worshiper is having the general recognition for excellent oral skills grading from A+ to B. However, a servant with excellent orals skills cannot be labeled "true" without other important essentials. They must be true by the meaning of worship and believe in the foundation of Demonsapienism in order to deal with the lifestyle that it entails. Like any other religion or belief, this philosophy lives by demonstration.

Prayer signifies commitment and spiritual centeredness. Some True Cock Worshipers will pray for God's undivided attention and there is no set requirement as to how often to pray. Servants of God pray for spiritual guidance but never for God's permission on whom to suck. They pray that Shem will bless them to be in the presence of the sub-deity in order to meet both sexual and spiritual obligations. Initiating prayer before anything is most important but showing appreciation and humility before the Lord is just as essential.

The term cock worship is simply interpreted as oral sex for those that use this phrase. Worship is a literal term for a True Cock Worshiper. A "blowjob" is never referred to as "True Cock Worship" as long as rituals are performed. Rituals demonstrate love, commitment and respect for God. Oral sex without penile rituals always will be semi-cock worship. A sacred tribute to the flesh of God offers respect, and one can receive various blessings as a result from semi-cock worship. The most instantaneous and general blessing is demonic ejaculation.

When a servant of God goes down between the legs of a deman, everything between the legs becomes an obligation accept for the anus. Not to make humor in this statement, but the rectum is an area that True Cock Worshipers avoid during worship for the reason that God is not an ass. Servants are to stay clear of this area because it is unsanitary. Demons in general do not know how to care for their ass, so servants must try to avoid this area during worship sessions. Even if a deman is familiar with the Middle Eastern technique for genital cleansing, avoid this area out of respect for God during worship.

For starters, never neglect the scrotum. When a servant is worshiping the penis, the scrotum is a privilege that must be inhaled. It becomes the place to smell the body of God. Even after a deman has worked hard, the smell of Shem while in a trance, is positively remarkable. All True Cock Worshipers make an obligation to smell, taste, lick, suck, stroke, kiss, and rub any part of the scrotum because it is a form of commitment.

Although the scent of a deman's scrotum might smell divine to a servant of God, they refuse to be humiliated with a prank, where a vessel keeper intentionally neglects his hygiene.

Demans should make a practice to have good, clean, daily hygiene; especially when they are being used for semi-cock or True Cock Worship.

The length and width of the penis is not relevant with a True Cock Worshiper. A circumcised cock is just as equally worthy as an uncircumcised cock. A cock that is in a permanent flaccid state is by far the greatest discovery. Penises that are permanently flaccid are the most valuable temples for the sub-deity to reside because it is the safest place under the sun.

When it comes to seeking oral worship, True Cock Worshipers make it a personal obligation at some point to adopt a flaccid penis and care for it for as long as possible. The spirit of the ultimate God always has a multitude of blessings residing within every motionless cock. Although God's presence appears completely absent and useless to a typical demon, the true test of time is to accommodate God in this state. Demans that are born without the ability to ever experience an erection might be useless to a Typical Cock Worshiper. However, a True Cock Worshiper seeks this kind of penis for ultimate blessings.

It is false to assume that a penis cannot become erect and is without worth. If a servant ever meets a paralyzed vessel keeper in his right state of mind, he or she is required to care for his penis until something forbids them from being together. Having compassion for the limp and impotent is a True Cock Worshiper's way to demonstrate honor to God and adhering to the voice of reasoning. Servants of God cannot achieve the greatest blessing until they have had the opportunity to worship a paralyzed penis. The most essential element about being a True Cock Worshiper is bowing down before the sub-deity in any worthy condition where he can be discovered.

The second rule a True Cock Worshiper must be able to accomplish is never or very seldom stop for anything other than swallowing saliva. Swallowing saliva is the only reason why there would need to be a pause during oral worship with the sub-deity. The sub-deity is always the focal point before anything else. A

True Cock Worshiper never loses sight of who receives the worship.

Servants are renowned for oral longevity. Their goal is to suck on the penis for as long as they can possibly endure. The average amount of time a servant will commit to oral practice is a minimum of forty-five minutes per session. Once they have committed to oral practice and without interruption from their volunteer, they might allow intercourse to happen afterward. True Cock Worshipers have no rules against having sex with their volunteers, but they will always attempt to have an experience first with the sub-deity.

Servants of God are good at not coming up for oxygen during oral sex because the mouth belongs to the sub-deity. Special breathing techniques provide oral longevity. They do not breathe out of the mouth because eighty percent of the time it is full and cannot receive oxygen. It becomes a skill that is similar to singing where the lungs have to be opened up. Breathing is done by inhaling long and deep through the nose, then filling the lungs up with oxygen and exhaling out of the nose. This technique, when applied to oral sex, take days or weeks of practice. The more a servant of God works on this technique, the more he or she will be able to develop excellent breathing abilities when a penis is in the mouth.

Demonsapiens that are new to True Cock Worship must first learn to manage their breathing because oral techniques are performed one after the other, with no breaks in between. Each technique is no less than eight minutes and no greater than twenty minutes. It is up to the servant to determine how long he intends to spend time with each technique. Ultimately, each session must amount to a minimum of one hundred and twenty minutes.

When a servant of God is performing a True Cock Worship session with their recipient, the timeframe for worship is much more intense. A True Cock Worshiping session can last for as long as two or more hours without stopping. Depending on the situation, a combination of techniques are used, some techniques more than others, and some not at all. True Cock Worshipers are determined about performing oral sex on the penis for as long as they can endure it. They are non-stop because they dream about having their own universe. They imagine developing a new world that will belong to them.

Worship sessions end often the same as they began. A servant finishes with a silent prayer facing the penis. It is common for recipients to witness servants literally coming from out of a spiritual state of drunkenness after penile worship. The heartbeat can drop significantly (60 beats per minute) caused by meditation. When this happens, a servant of God needs time to reconnect with their surroundings. It is important not to distract them because the heart needs time to return to a normal pace. Recipients should be extra sensitive to this process and remain silent during this time until spoken to.

True Cock Worship requires a lot of mental, physical and emotional endurance by someone who is willing to become a demonic sacrifice. A lot of time is committed to True Cock

Worshiping, and that is why so few demans are worthy. Both the recipient and the servant of God can experience the most intense kind of worship.

True Cock Worshipers do not specify penile rituals but each session generally does begin with a deep cleansing and massage, whereas with semi-cock worship it does not. Equally nurtured are the scrotum and penis during the ritual process. Deep cleansing and message preparations can last up to forty-five minutes but no less than twenty minutes. Recipients should not be offended when a servant cleans and pampers their cock. Some recipients claim that the cleansing process is more enjoyable.

Demonsapiens that seek the same oral abilities as True Cock Worshipers have the potential to learn these same techniques. However, a number of expectations are required to demonstrate a demon's (both male and female demonsapiens) potential. New servants of God are most likely to have the right mindset for worshiping from beginning to end. For example, servant is never supposed to expect praise from the receiver. Oral sex is purely a spiritual, mental and physical passion.

A True Cock Worshiper's oral skills is nothing spectacular. It is not as though they have three tongues or special abilities. Anyone that loves to suck on a cock might say they have the best technique, yet all techniques generally are the same. Much like oral experts, servants of God are also very committed to the act of oral sex.

Unfortunately, not all penises are the same, and that is why many kinds of techniques are necessary. Servants know generally how to perform at least eighteen oral techniques but a minimum of eleven techniques should be performed during each worship session. Depending on the circumstances, such situations as having erectile dysfunction or being extremely well endowed are reasons to make modifications. If a servant can find an eligible vessel keeper, all eleven techniques should be practiced in one session.

Typical Cock Worshipers with great oral abilities already will have mastered many of these techniques. Some will not master any more than seven techniques. They are considered sexually incompetent. Demonsapiens that do not want to be sexually incompetent will learn how to do all eighteen techniques. While plenty other demons around the world know how to perform a variety of other techniques, only the following eighteen listed is considered to be True Cock Worship.

Naturally, not everyone will have the ability to do some of the following techniques because some are considered deep throating. There are five levels of throat skills that ranges from not intense to very intense.

Technique one is "The Infancy Phase." This is where the mouth operates as a womb for the penis. God, being the infant in a flaccid state, is considered the Infancy Phase. A new servant would begin by sucking on the whole penis (if possible) just as a baby sucks on a pacifier. This is continuous without stopping.

Continue to breathe out of the nose while consuming the whole penis in a flaccid state, if possible. The goal is to place all of the sub-deity into the mouth, as if to swallow him. The penis should be completely inside of the mouth, down to the pubic hairs or base of the penis. If a servant is unable to swallow the full body of God in a flaccid state due to the length of the penis, he or she is forgiven.

Whenever the sub-deity is present, it is the duty of a servant to keep him safe. The goal is to keep the penis warm and in the womb for as long as possible. Continue to suck on the lesser god in the Infancy Phase and never release or let him fall from out of the womb (mouth). Try not to use the hands. If the penis falls out of the mouth, maneuver your head and mouth to bring him back into the safe place of warmth. Swallow the secretions of pre-cum and suck for as long as it takes so that God can become erect (or not). This technique is graded as level two (mildly intense) on a True Cock Worshiper's intensity scale of Five Throat Skills.

The second technique is "The Gliss." As a new servant begins to experience the growth of God within the womb, he or she will naturally produce more secretions. The Gliss technique helps manage the secretions coming from the mouth. As saliva builds up, beginning servants will feel the urge to spit, drool or slobber on the penis. Demans in general might appreciate when spit, drool and slobber is running down the shaft of their cock and onto their scrotum. Typical Cock Worshipers do not have rules for spitting, drooling and slobbering, but they do not believe that they are worshiping God, either.

True Cock Worshipers, on the other hand, have a completely different perspective about caring for the penis. Spitting, drooling and slobbering is very disrespectful since the penis is a sacred deity. Servants of God do have a wild side, but it is never during a True Cock Worship or semi-cock worship session. Spitting, drooling, slobbering, and vomiting is acceptable barbarianism but these acts are saved for non-worship related encounters.

If a demonsapien wants to become a True Cock Worshiper, they must first learn how to re-think oral sex by respecting the sub-deity and using techniques that are not demeaning to the spirit of God. This technique is graded a level one (not intense) on a True Cock Worshiper's intensity scale of Five Throat Skills.

The third technique is "The Reminisce." This technique allows a servant to meditate on every millimeter of God no matter what the shape or size of the penis is. The Reminisce technique begins at the head of the penis. Slowly moving down the base of the penis, the mouth stops every quarter of an inch to rest. The whole penis, if possible, remains inside the mouth for five seconds or more before sliding down further.

It is a very deep and intense skill that requires a servant to be in meditation mode. The best time to begin this technique is about twenty-five minutes into an oral session. At this time, a True Cock Worshiper is ready to consume all of God in a fully erect state. The Reminisce is done as often as possible and for as long as the servant can withstand. Meditate on every element of the body of God by focusing on length, thickness, veins and anything else able to recall with the mouth and tongue. Once the base of the sub-deity becomes completely consumed (or at least half way consumed), move back up to the head of the penis slowly. Engulf the sub-deity with aggressiveness by returning straight back into the mouth, or throat if possible, with one full stroke. Once the servant's mouth is at the base again, he or she uses the up and down oral motion. Sometimes the penis will feel tiny thrusting coming from the back of the servant's throat. This technique is done as many times as possible and is graded a level five (very intense) on a True Cock Worshiper's intensity scale of Five Throat Skills.

The fourth technique is "The Greeting Stroke." The Greeting Stroke is rapid oral thrusting that Typical Cock Worshipers would call deep throating. True Cock Worshipers, however, do not use the term deep throating. The fully erect body of God is taken into the mouth and down the throat as quickly and deeply as possible. Naturally, secretions will develop from this act alone. A servant should not stop unless to breathe improperly through the mouth, blow the nose or to swallow saliva. This technique is done as many times as possible and is graded a level five (very intense) on a True Cock Worshiper's intensity scale of Five Throat Skills.

The fifth technique is "The Charm." The mouth engulfs the penis at the base to tickle with the tongue (if possible). It is a throat skill technique that is done by moving the tongue from side to side while at the base of the penis. In some cases, breathing out of the mouth is possible, but the diameter of the penis head determines if it is feasible or not. Any deman that has up to an average sized penis in length and girth is most ideal for this technique. Penises above the normal length and girth – for example, eight-and-three-quarter inches and above in length or four-and-a-half inches in girth or more – might not be feasible for the Charm technique. Do not forget to breath in and out of the nose. This technique is done as many times as possible and is graded a level four (intense) on a True Cock Worshiper's intensity scale of Five Throat Skills.

The sixth technique is "The Muff." This technique is the most basic and common approach for any demonsapien that is learning how to orally worship. The Muff technique is for concentrating primarily on the head of the penis. Inverted lips are wrapped around the head and sucked on for as long as possible. This technique does not require deep throating skills therefore a minimum of eight minutes must be committed. It is graded a level one (not intense) on a True Cock Worshiper's intensity scale of Five Throat Skills.

The seventh technique is, "The Gasp." Of all the techniques, the Gasp technique is the most important one of all. Suffocating one's nose in the scrotum of a volunteer or recipient opens up an endless world of knowledge about them. It is a known fact that True Cock Worshipers can find out many things based on the scent of the deman being used. True Cock Worshipers can know how long ago a deman showered or bathed. They can know if he had sex with a partner prior to engaging with the servant, even after he has taken a shower. Servants can know a deman's diet based on the scent of his scrotum. They can also tell if he is on medication, but do not be alarmed because very little of this matters. This technique is an obligation that a True Cock Worshiper has with an unspoken ability.

The Gasp is a requirement for all True Cock Worshipers and is always done before ending a worship session under the right circumstances. True Cock Worshipers absolutely must inhale the scent of the sub-deity for their soul to be complete. They must kiss and smell the full body of God by rubbing their noses over the cock and into scrotum. True Cock Worshipers make a point to inhale every part of the sub-deity. They will not come up for fresh air until after eight minutes. This technique does not have a grade on a True Cock Worshiper's intensity scale because it does not involve the throat.

The eighth technique is "The Gad." There is no exact science about how to do the Gad technique, but the scrotum is not to be neglected. Sucking the scrotum is carefully done by using the lips. The tongue is maneuvered over the scrotum alternating with random gentle sucking. It should last for no less than eight minutes and should occur between other techniques.

The ninth technique is "The Boa." The penis has to be somewhat erect in order to execute successfully. Servants begin by squeezing the shaft of God with their lips. They continue by lip squeezing down to the base, or as far down as possible. When it is time to come up, the servant will suck while squeezing lips and moving up the shaft. Beginning once again at the head of the penis, they move back down the shaft. This time it is with tight inverted lips as if to be too tight for the penis to enter the mouth. This combination lasts for as long as possible or for a minimum of eight minutes. This technique is graded a level four (intense) on a True Cock Worshiper's intensity scale of Five Throat Skills.

Hands are generally not a part of the skill during a worship session, but when the sub-deity is uncommonly long, it is an obligation not to neglect any part of him.

The tenth technique is "The Wring." Both hands are wrapped around the body of God. The hands gently twist around the shaft in opposite directions at the same time. If both hands are not necessary, one is used to cup the scrotum, while the other hand wraps around the shaft and gently twisting up and down. The goal is always to keep the sub-deity safe and warm. Whether needing to use both hands or not, use the mouth to engulf as much of the lesser god as possible. If it is too difficult, try to consume at least five inches for starters. Continue worshiping for no less than eight minutes at a time. This technique is graded a level three (moderately intense) on a True Cock Worshiper's intensity scale of Five Throat Skills. It requires multitasking and coordination abilities more than throat skill.

Technique eleven is "The Path," and the penis must be fully erect and upright in order to accomplish. This technique begins at the scrotum while the penis is inside the mouth. The tip of the tongue runs up the center of the shaft. This is done three to four times between other techniques or for a total of eight minutes nonstop. It is graded a level two (mildly intense) on a True Cock Worshiper's intensity scale of Five Throat Skills.

The twelfth technique is "The Pillar." This is where the lips glide across the penis as if to mimic how a harmonica plays. The penis can be either erect or in a flaccid state and resting to the left or to the right. Both sides of the penis should benefit from this technique. The mouth and tongue are to be used for maneuvering rather than hands. Continue this technique for no less than eight minutes at a time. This technique does not have a grade on a level of intensity because it is not a throat skill.

The thirteenth technique is "The Totter." The penis does not need to be completely inside the mouth nor fully erect. The Totter, by the force of the tongue, allows the penis to shift inside the mouth from side to side. This technique should be no less than eight minutes at a time and can be done in between other techniques. The Totter is not on the scale of intensity because it is not a throat skill.

The fourteenth technique is, "The Remora." The Remora is when the penis is inside the mouth or at least a quarter of an inch or more down the throat, resting for approximately thirty seconds or longer. This is the only technique where knowing how to breath correctly is crucial. If this technique is executed successfully, the servant will remain in an unmoving and tranquil position for at least thirty seconds or longer while the recipient/volunteer remains very still and unresponsive. Those who will be able to perform this technique will learn to hold longer, move the tongue around, and suck on the penis, all at the same time while at the base of the penis. Some vessel keepers are able to feel a hummer or flutter coming from the back of the servant's throat.

Unfortunately, not every demonsapien will be able to do this particular technique do due having a congenital disorder, small throat passage, or large tonsils. Demonsapiens born with physical conditions such as these will have a legitimate excuse for not being able to perform many of these techniques.

In time, new servants can perform this technique for up to one minute or longer by simply using stored oxygen in the lungs. This technique is graded a level five (very intense) on a True Cock Worshiper's intensity scale of Five Throat Skills.

The fifteenth technique is "The Tapering." For the first time, the forearm is used. It is very direct and to the point. The right forearm rests over the top of the recipient/volunteer's pelvic bone area. The left hand cups the scrotum while pressure is placed on top of the pelvis. The forearm rocks the pelvic area back and forth while the penis bobbles into the mouth. If the servant is left handed the position can be reversed. As long as it is moderately fast, it can be very effective. This technique can be accomplished within eight minutes without stopping. It is graded a level two (mildly intense) on the intensity scale of Five Throat Skills.

The sixteenth technique is "The Ebb." The mouth of the servant moves in a constant circular motion on the penis. Moving slowly down the shaft creates a most unusual sensation that feels not necessarily pleasurable but different. The Ebb is one of the only techniques that does not have to be for more than eight minutes at a time. It is graded a level one on the intensity scale of Five Throat Skills.

The seventeenth technique is "The Kaman." Ironically, the Kaman technique is actually not very common because it can cause those with very sensitive gag reflexes to vomit. This technique is not for the common demon because most will not attempt it. Typical Cock Worshipers are known to comply with this technique, especially when it is initiated by a dominant deman. In fact, some of them will beg for it. True Cock Worshipers, however, are leaders. The only way they accomplish their skills is with lots of practice.

When a cock is too thick to swallow or take down the throat, the Kaman is the best way to express one's dedication to God. This technique requires True Cock Worshipers to slam brutally their tonsils directly into contact with the head of a very thick penis for a long period. Eventually, the Kaman will make the tonsils strong, allowing the servant to do every technique that requires throat skills.

Deman recipients/volunteers do not need to feel pleasure through the Kaman because they are not the focus. They might think it is a pointless act because they experience no joy in it. However, it does not matter if they understand this technique or not. Attempt to do it for as long as possible or for no less than eight minutes. It is graded a level five (very intense) on a True Cock Worshiper's intensity scale of Five Throat Skills.

The eighteenth technique is "The Kia." This technique is always the last one to be performed because it is a way to thank the recipient. Never use this technique with a volunteer unless he has been faithful for over a long period. The Kia always comes at the end of a True Cock Worship or semi-cock worship session. It is a way of thanking the recipient (or long-term volunteer) that was used as a sacrifice to God. He must remain silently still on his back throughout the session for at least 190 minutes to receive this form of appreciation. The physical position a recipient/volunteer chooses will determine if this technique will work. If he sits upright or stands rather than lying, the Kia technique will not be possible to do.

Thanking should only come after 190 minutes of patience and does not have to last but fifteen seconds. Servants must already be in between the legs as the deman lay on his back. The servant's arms have to be stretched all the way underneath the back of the recipient, as if to hug him. His back is then massaged while giving the Greeting Stroke for a grand finale. This technique follows prayer, but it is optional. It is done only if the servant wants to say thank you. It is graded a level three (intense) on the intensity scale of Five Throat Skills.

Swallowing semen is something that Typical Cock Worshipers often do to satisfy their deman masters. However, the thought process with True Cock Worshipers is different. It might come as a surprise, but True Cock Worshipers always spit out semen. The reason why they always spit is primarily to remind the vessel keeper that he is not the focal point nor does he have the ability to control the servant. The servant of God is always in control, and a deman should never forget it.

It is also up to the servant whether to swallow the sperm of their recipient. If a True Cock Worshiper does decide to swallow a recipient's semen, it could ruin everything. He might become confused about his role after such an act.

When there is a hard ejaculation, it is possible that semen can enter the mouth, exiting out the nose. Semen can clog the nasal passage causing all oxygen to block at an instant. Should this happen, spit out the semen and blow out the nose.

A very large amount of time is dedicated to the penis and with complete liberty. Sometimes having tonsils has its disadvantages. Some demons have a difficult time passing a cock down the throat depending on the size of the tonsils.

There is much debate about the removal of tonsils. Some experts say that tonsils are there for a reason and should not be removed. Tonsils are like filters that collect and prevent infection from spreading throughout the body. Experts say tonsils prevent infections from travelling throughout the bloodstream. Unfortunately, if a servant is prone to getting tonsillitis, strep throat, or other such throat conditions, it will be difficult to have a successful experience with the sub-deity in the way a servant wants.

Being able to swallow semen is mind over matter more than anything. It is a decision the servant makes. Understanding the pleasures of one's taste palette is what determines whether a servant will swallow or not. The mind has to be willing and ready to explore this part of a deman. New cock worshipers that have never tried to swallow semen or have had a hard time with the concept, can do so with the right mindset.

The tongue is a taste palette tapping into a part of the brain that allows one to accept the pleasures of taste, smell, color and textures. It can be different from one demonsapien to the next. Some have taste palettes that are aroused by sweet and bitter foods. Others have taste palettes that enjoy salty and spicy foods. Once a cock worshiper is able to identify their pleasure, the brain immediately will decide and will react on the given impulse to swallow or not.

Unless the servant knows the diet of the deman, he or she cannot be sure what to expect as far as semen taste. Vessel keepers do not realize that having a poor diet can affect the taste of their sperm. Sperm is known to taste salty with carnivores. If the deman is consuming more than 12 lbs. of red meat a week, naturally he will taste like salt because the animals he ate required sodium and chloride in their diet.

When a new servant of God discovers that they do not like the taste of semen, then they should not ever attempt to do it again. If the taste continues to linger on the tongue, gargle 1 tablespoon of undiluted apple cider vinegar for 8 seconds in the mouth, and this will alleviate the aftertaste. Do this as often as needed. Swallowing semen is not a requirement for a True Cock Worshiper, but it is with most Typical Cock Worshipers.

As all know, the mouth was designed for consumption and swallowing. Allowing a deman to ejaculate inside the mouth is always a great blessing. If an eligible deman allows his penis inside a True Cock Worshiper's mouth, it is thought to be an honor. Servants of God usually allow this act but it is a step further if one decides to swallow. Swallowing signifies submission and love for the recipient or volunteer(s) therefore it is discouraged. When a servant establishes a serious relationship with a recipient or volunteer, he or she might declare this commitment by swallowing semen, but it is not guaranteed.

Swallowing semen always makes a stronger and statement because actions speak louder than words. It is a decision that is solely based on surrendering dominance and is not to be taken lightly. Servants of God also do not swallow semen for the following reasons.

When a deman does not act responsible enough to protect his penis from harm, it demonstrates that he does not care about his health. Semen is not suppose to have a bad smell, but if it does, it could be a clear sign that something is wrong with his health. When semen smells like rotten seafood, then it is a clear sign that your vessel keeper might have an STD. However, it is common that semen smell like aluminum.

Semen comes in various densities and textures. It can have the same consistency of mucus and sometimes appears thick or stringy. The color of healthy semen ranges from milky white to clear and are in the safe range for swallowing. Always avoid consuming yellow semen, because this color is not in the safe range for swallowing. If a deman's semen is brown, it becomes a health concern and might mean that blood is in it. In fact, neglected is the physical condition of this penis.

When a servant of God is new to True Cock Worship, they should expect neck, jaw and lower back discomforts as well as physical exhaustion. True Cock Worshipers get tired, especially when they are sharing the space with a self-centered deman. It is important not to dress in the way that seduces them or sends mixed messages. If the mind is weak, wear a chastity belt and leave the key at home. There is a differentiation between the physical, mental and spiritual aspects of a deman. True servants know the differences between sub-deity, god, God, deman, demon, demonica, servant of God, and the voice of reason.

Individuals with low testosterone cannot be cured but they can be treated because it is a medical condition. It is important that all vessel keepers be chemically balanced both physically and mentally for oral sex. When they are not, the servant will discern it and advise them to visit a urologist. True Cock Worshipers have the ability to detect whether or not an individual has a chemical imbalance in his brain. The servant might not know that it is low testosterone but he or she can know when something is not right psychologically. A vessel keeper's mentality and psychological wellbeing is always in the best interest of the parties involved.

There are specific requirements True Cock Worshipers must accept when they have received an honest vision through prayer. The voice of reasoning might tell them to seek a deman that suffers from premature ejaculation. Recipient eligibility is very strict and should not be compromised. A True Cock Worshiper also will have to accept that he or she might call for someone that is with erectile dysfunction, three inches erect, nine inches long, seven inches in diameter, circumcised, uncircumcised, penis curved to the left, penis curved to the right, upward erect, downward erect, without piercings, with piercings, with a mole, with a birth mark, with scars, with two penises, intersexed individuals with a penis or a demonica with a large clitoris. The voice of reasoning will direct a servant of God to search for various kinds of recipients when praying for one.

Servants should be honest with their recipient or volunteer(s) from the beginning. They are never to lead on anyone that appears emotionally invested. They should never put themselves in a dangerous situation for worship. A servant should never feel guilty when he or she does not feel permitted to use an individual for worship due to his poor mental state. Those being used should have a clear understanding about their purpose. Once a servant of God finds a recipient or volunteer(s) that understands and respects his place as a demonic sacrifice, True Cock Worshipers will be obligated to fulfill all or most of the acts in order to receive God's blessings.

Chapter 11
DUTIES AND COMPLEXITIES OF RECIPIENTS

Finding a recipient with the right mentality seems to be almost impossible, yet it is necessary for every servant of God to seek one. Recipients are more difficult to come by because they are required to remain both sexually submissive and mentally stable. Sexually deprived and submissive demans are most ideal for True Cock Worship, because they are not only faithful but dependable.

Servants of God will choose a recipient to fulfill True Cock Worshiping sessions for over a long period of time. Undeclared relationships with recipients naturally develop but primarily through the sacredness and holiness of the sub-deity. Since both the servant and recipient need each other for sex, this makes for a harmonious balance.

True Cock Worshipers will take advantage of their recipients in more than one way, which decreases their blessings, confuses the relationship status, and makes finding a replacement more difficult. On the other hand, if a spouse is a recipient or is also a servant of God, it is acceptable and in fact one of the greatest blessings that a True Cock Worshiper can have.

Recipients are valuable intimate necessities that servants depend on to meet with the sub-deity. They are the ultimate sacrifice to God. They have a respect for the rituals that are performed on them as well as respect for the True Cock Worshiper's belief, even if different from their own. Some recipients believe that being used as a peace offering to God grants them their own kingdom. Recipient are the only ones that have the right to know the details of penile rituals. It is disrespectful to the recipient and to God for a True Cock Worshiper to discuss the ritual process with a stranger.

It is important that servants keep images of their recipient's penis for meditation. The use of rituals is essential to the process of worship and must be included when using a recipient. Meditation is a way to properly channel how to satisfy the sub-deity without words from the vessel keeper. Meditation enables a servant to discern the sub-deity's needs and become one with him. Once a servant is able to succeed at satisfying the needs of the sub-deity and without the direction of the vessel keeper, he or she can receive other blessings that extend beyond demonic ejaculation. There is no set requirement on how often to meditate, but it is encouraged to do so at least once a day, especially before meeting with the recipient. Meditation is good for every reason but it is not a requirement with volunteers. It is not necessary to meditate prior to a session with a volunteer because a servant might ask the deman what he likes sexually, after a semi-cock worship session.

When there is no recipient or volunteer, a True Cock Worshiper will resort to idolizing pictures of penises as an alternative. Photos and illustrations are for meditation and decorating penis alters. They also accept the generous donations that come from demans that are willing to share pictures of their penis. Looking at several cocks in honor of the sub-deity is a way of showing dedication and appreciation for God.

Servants do not accept headshots or full body shots from their recipient because he is not the focal point. They would prefer to take photographs of their recipient's cock. When it is not possible, a servant will accept whatever photograph provided and if necessary, cut off the head or any part that is not the sub-deity.

While being a recipient has its benefits, emotional burdens come with being used as a vessel keeper for God. They are likely to endure a number of emotional challenges as a result from being used as a demonic sacrifice. Most might have to deal with mental challenges that requires an emotional disconnection.

Recipients must successfully be able to separate themselves psychologically from their penis to become a physical sacrifice. Some vessel keepers will need to learn how to have non-critical and non-judgmental opinions in the process. To be the perfect sacrifice, a recipient must demonstrate an honest act of humility and unselfishness.

Reciprocation is not an option with a demonic sacrifice, therefore hostility and frustrations are bound to occur at the expense of his charity. He might experience an emotional attachment as the testosterone releases or find himself susceptible to developing a growing frustration in the mental chase. Recipients might become offended knowing that their penis is being worshiped but not them. They might build resentment knowing that they cannot speak or touch during a session.

True Cock Worshipers benefit by having one penis to worship and having the recipient to sacrifice. Their recipient does not have the right to request special kinds of sexual gratification, nor can he criticize performance or even techniques. A recipient can caress his own ego by knowing that he will be the only one that will receive the greatest amount of pleasure. He can accept this way of thinking as a positive mental strategy that will help him retract infatuation for the servant of God.

It is highly recommended that recipients have a significant other, or a conflict of interest could develop. They might not be able to maintain a healthy state of mind if they forget that they are just a demonic sacrifice. Vessel keepers are encouraged to have a relationship aside from the servant because it gives them stability.

A recipient must have a personal life or relationship of his own. However, if he is afraid of commitment, he might be susceptible to believing that he is already in a relationship with the True Cock Worshiper. He might have come to the illusion that a mutual relationship with the servant has developed. This misunderstanding could harm his opportunity for connecting with another demonsapien.

Some of the issues that a recipient has but might not reveal to a True Cock Worshiper would be, not being able to maintain a healthy relationship outside of the intimacy he has with the servant. He might solely depend on him or her to fulfill his sexual needs, avoid emotional commitments, not develop emotional connections with other demonsapiens, or enter a serious relationship with someone who forbids sharing him. Any of these issues could automatically make a potential recipient ineligible.

Recipients are not required to have the same spiritual beliefs; in fact, they do not even have to understand Demonsapienism. The only requirements a recipient needs is to be physically available and to always have respect for the servant of God during worship sessions.

They are often indirectly interviewed before determining if they qualify. The interview is done unbeknownst to the vessel keeper and usually consists of a series of questions regarding his spiritual, physical, and mental stability. If the servant does not believe the deman is ideal, then he will not be used.

Potential recipients cannot struggle with or develop substance abuse problems. They cannot be possessive because it interprets as being mentally unstable. The flesh of a potential recipient must be clean and disease free to be a good sacrifice to God. In addition, he cannot be a sex addict, suicidal or obsessed with the servant because he will become a problem rather than a solution.

Recipients are not eligible after intentionally cutting, burning, or other such acts that would cause serious injury or permanent damage to the penis. Penile abuse will never be an acceptable act nor will it ever be the motive for a semi-cock worship or True Cock Worship session.

There are many reasons why a True Cock Worshiper is careful about choosing a recipient. He must first be honest about his sexual history to be eligible. If he cannot be honest about his sexual past, then he becomes a high risk to all the parties involved. It is not important how many partners he has had but rather how careful he has been with his promiscuity. Even if a recipient chooses not to tell the truth about having an STD, a True Cock Worshiper will know if he is lying. They will listen to the voice of reason, pray and meditate on the honesty of this deman.

Much respect goes to the potential recipient who, before anything begins, is able to be honest and admit to having an STD that is incurable but treatable. The way to prove one's worthiness is by being tested for every STD and earning the trust of a True Cock Worshiper that also provides the same type of tests. Another reason a recipient should be honest is to confirm that he is eligible for oral worship without a condom.

Demans are usually rejected if they are married or seriously invested with someone. It is primarily due to their unavailability to make time. However, servants will perform oral worship with them as long as their significant other is aware of it.

Condoms are used for oral worship in every situation when the voice of reason tells them to.

True Cock Worshipers test for STD's as often as every three to six months to prove that they are disease free. Both the recipient and servant should present no less than a 2-month current and original document showing that they are clear of all diseases and viruses. If a vessel keeper contracts an STD after becoming a recipient, he must be honest enough to tell the servant. Under such circumstances, and depending on the severity of the virus/disease, sessions will not continue without protection and not until the recipient is treated.

Recipients generally receive True Cock Worship sessions by one servant. It is rare that one have a True Cock Worshiper, then be approached yet again by another servant of God asking for True Cock Worshiping sessions. If a recipient has more than one servant, then he must literally enjoy living on his back just for sex, because it is uncommon for them to have more than one. Two or more True Cock Worshipers can share the same deman, especially if he is in a committed relationship with one that allows it. He has the right to accept or decline the offer. If a recipient accepts a second True Cock Worshiper, time with the sub-deity will have to be equally shared between both servants but, not necessarily at the same time.

Recipients are required to surrender their sexual rights over to the servant during worship sessions. What True Cock Worshipers cannot control is when a recipient reaches climax and ejaculates. If he decides to ejaculate during the session, he is required to make it known first by saying, "God is imminent" just before finishing. After a recipient reaches climax, it does not mean that the session is over. The servant will not stop; in fact, he or she might spit out the semen (or swallow). The servant will continue on with oral worship as long as they are under a meditative state.

Recipients do not get to speak during True Cock Worship sessions because it is rude, selfish, disrespectful and distracting for the servant. They are only allowed to speak if feeling sick, having discomfort, pain, or needing to ejaculate. During a True Cock Worship session, the recipient also has the right to say, "stop" if he becomes uncomfortable. He should not have to give an explanation. If the word "stop" is used, the servant of God must obey it. This word comes directly from the sub-deity and communicates what his vessel feels, servants therefore must obey this command. The moment a recipient speaks without a valid reason, the servant will immediately have to end the session.

Once a recipient becomes eligible for True Cock Worship he can fall asleep, yawn, sneeze, cough, laugh, cry, snore, moan, adjust himself, lock knees, curl toes, flex toes, point toes, uncontrollably shake, lie down, sit up, stand, scratch, clear throat, eat a breath mint, chew gum, watch TV with volume on mute or read a book during the worship session. Recipients are forbidden, however, to touch the servant, have animals present, urinate, eat anything other than breath mints, smoke, drink (including water), speak, listen to music, talk on the phone, text message, use laptop, burp, vomit, spit/hack, pass gas/fart, thrust/rock pelvis, help, assist, conduct, direct, instruct, or manage the session. Recipients cannot touch the servant of God during a worship session. If they do touch and continue to touch the servant, they become no longer useful since they cannot respect the rules of conduct.

Sometimes the recipient will wear a blindfold during a worship session so that he cannot see what the servant is doing to him. He can feel what is happening and should fantasize by using his imagination. It is perfectly natural to dream or fantasize about someone or wish to have a sexual experience with. If a recipient feels tempted to touch the servant, he needs to let it be known beforehand. By doing this, he is being honest about his weakness but still wants to be useful. He also opens himself up to vulnerability and possibility having his wrists and ankles bound. This act alone would demonstrate an act of commitment and respect for the dominant servant of God. A recipient must not only respect the rules and beliefs of a True Cock Worshiper, but no matter what, he should be thankful. He could then remain useful with restraints, to avoid interruptions during the worship sessions.

It is common that a recipient develop a growing fascination for the servant. Unless he is a True Vagina Worshiper, he should not expect anything in return on either an emotional or physical level. A recipient's responsibility is to simply maintain a healthy relationship with the servant of God.

He can experience being one with the sub-deity when his mind is not in a dominant position and also find himself spiritually enlightened. A deman with this amount of potential could be worth more in the future such as a monogamous relationship.

True Cock Worshipers understand that family, school, and work sometimes can make these arrangements inconvenient. They understand that it is not possible to commit to every single worship session, but communication is the key with such relations. An open line of communication within the relationship is a common courtesy between both the recipient and the servant.

When a recipient abandons his responsibility or neglects to communicate, this is a very serious decision. True Cock Worshipers have a mourning process for this reason. Some leave and some return, but in worst cases some die. Recipients have the tendency to disappear without a warning or an explanation. In many cases, a recipient will disappear without notice. In this case, they are permitted to have 14 days of personal time to recuperate from what could have been an intense worship session. A True Cock Worshiper will pray for their recipient's wellbeing and remain faithful to his generosity.

A recipient can neglect a servant, for whatever reason, for up to 14 days. His reasons will remain unknown until contacted but he does not have to give an explanation. If the recipient contacts the servant on the 14th day, he can be taken back without an explanation. If he wants to sit down and explain himself, then allow him, but whatever he says it should not be held against him.

If the recipient does not return by the 15th day, the mourning process must begin and end after 90 days. Should the vessel keeper return in the middle of the mourning process, he has to wait until the mourning is over. If he returns after a year or more, he must be punished by waiting 90 days and 180 more days for every year that he abandoned his obligation. In most cases, the recipient already will have been replaced. Before seeking a new recipient, a True Cock Worshiper adds 90 days more to mourn, for every year that they had their recipient. No matter how short-lived his time was, he will be mourned for 90 days and replaced with someone new through prayer and meditation.

If the recipient dies and passes on to the second Dimension of Demonic Existence, he will automatically be elevated to a god-like status. A picture of the demonsapien's face will be added to the altar where the servant of God kept photos solely of his penis. One photograph of the recipient's face is displayed on the penis alter because he his dead. He has moved on to the next life and is noted as a kindred spirit.

Chapter 12
DUTIES AND COMPLEXITIES OF VOLUNTEERS

Volunteers are temporary substitutes that True Cock Worshipers use to fulfill partial duties called semi-cock worship. There is a high risk in using a volunteer, and that is why a great deal of time and effort goes into seeking the right recipient.

Generally, volunteers are clueless about the possible opportunities they can have by simply knowing a True Cock Worshiper. They might not be familiar with Demonsapienology, however, knowing this raises fascination as well as their desire to know firsthand the oral abilities of a "True" Cock Worshiper.

Volunteers are sometimes good at raising interesting questions about the meaning of being "true" as opposed to being "typical."

It is pertinent that potential volunteers understand the sexual side as well as the spiritual side, since some of it can become quite complex. Getting involved with a True Cock Worshiper in general might be risky because their lifestyle sometimes teeters on the borderline of polyandry. Not every deman is emotionally capable of being a part of this lifestyle, but some are. They will wait around for an opportunity to have an experience with a true servant of God. Unfortunately, when a volunteer starts to become emotionally attached, he is prone to getting hurt because a servant's position is to not fall in lust.

Some volunteers might have a difficult time understanding their position as they come to learn about others. Servants are known to have sexual intercourse with their volunteers when the feelings are mutual. Some might end up abandoned after one session of semi-cock worship because the servant does not want to accumulate a large number of them.

Vessel keepers should never feel threatened or inferior to other volunteers. Some might assume that they are competing for the servant's attention, when in actuality they are not. They should never take it personal or believe that they have been discarded due to another deman. Volunteers are competing with the voice of reason that tells a servant to find one eligible recipient.

True Cock Worshipers might abandon their volunteer(s) to concentrate on finding one recipient to obtain the fullness of True Cock Worship. Their minds are primarily focused on being able to self-indulge the craft with one eligible deman who will embrace a dominant servant. True Cock Worshipers strive at maintaining the ability to focus on what is best for their lifestyle but it comes with both emotional and sexual risks.

Potential volunteers can and should explore this lifestyle if they want. Often times a volunteer will end up a valuable acquaintance and remain faithful to the servant for many years. If a deman wishes to participate in such a lifestyle, he must prove himself to be emotionally centered, confident, trustworthy and honest.

The voice of reason might also tell a True Cock Worshiper not to have anyone for an unknown period. This means that it is their time to self-reflect upon what is best for their spiritual wellbeing. Sometimes oral worship can cloud the mind of a servant. He or she might lose sight of what is most important and this is why they must trust the voice of reasoning. There must be a balance between worship, prayer and meditation; it is the only way to live for God.

There is a slight difference between recipients as opposed to volunteers. Blowjobs are done with volunteers for practice. This oral practice makes a servant ready and prepared for their recipient. Sometimes volunteers are used for a True Cock Worshiper's selfish desires but long-term commitments are not expected. It is rare to find volunteers single, available, and not interested in someone who will suck their cock at no expense. They are easy to come by and can be replaced in a heartbeat but only used when a servant of God has no recipient. Most of the time volunteers do not know that they are being used for semi-cock worship because True Cock Worshipers have spiritual views that are not important to them.

Recipients and volunteers are not to be used for personal gains such as material possession, prestige, wealth, fame, looks or age. These are irrelevant qualities that have nothing to do with cock worship and are not the focal point. True Cock Worshipers have a separate obligation that is solely based on spirituality. They require spiritual compatibility, and this is what sets them far apart from Typical Cock Worshipers.

Every so often, a True Cock Worshiper will run into a spiritual wall. A spiritual wall means having to deal with an aggressive and dominant deman. Sharing an uncomfortable space with the wrong deman is the risk a servant of God takes without prayer and meditation. It is important they pray before meeting up at least an hour prior to every new sexual encounter.

If prayer is not done prior to meeting with a new volunteer, spiritual warfare of some sort should be expected.

A True Cock Worshiper will determine whether a deman is mentally, emotionally and physically adequate based on this evidence. They are sensitive to spiritual conflicts with other demonsapiens. Negative characteristics are revealed through the voice of reasoning. True Cock Worshipers recognize and try to avoid obvious signs of negative characteristics while other demons do not.

A significant amount of uneasiness can come after using a volunteer that never fit the requirements. Prayer and meditation would allow the voice of reasoning to be heard by presenting second thoughts and/or doubts about a him. There can be plenty of warning signs, but the voice of reason is the confirmation that all True Cock Worshipers wait for. The consequences can be detrimental if a servant decides to settle for any type of vessel keeper, especially when the voice of reason discourages it.

Demonsapienism & True Cock Worship

Just because a deman possesses a penis does not mean the sub-deity is present. God is only present when its vessel keeper acknowledges Shem's spirit. The sub-deity must be acknowledged and respected, or the volunteer becomes ineligible for semi-cock worship. Insulting the spirit of the sub-deity is intolerant. The spirit of God cannot live in the body of a penis with a deman that has negative opinions about his genitals.

There might be such cases where a True Cock Worshiper has not prayed and might attempt to physically seduce another demon by groping him without permission. In some cases, a servant of God that lives life without prayer could lead them to getting raped, which is not the positive side of semi-cock worship.

The nature of all demons is to destroy one another either nicely or maliciously but always deliberately. Prayer and meditation helps reveal malicious vessel keepers prior to every new experience and helps True Cock Worshipers recognize when a deman has been wrongfully chosen. Prayer and meditation helps discern incompatibility. Acknowledging the voice of reason tells us that we have the cognitive ability to make the right decision.

A true servant of God has no business being in the presence of a deman that continues to show contempt for his penis. Should he disvalue his penis in any way, shape, or form, it is a direct insult to God and all of Shem's creation. It is easy to tell when a deman has no respect for the sub-deity or his penis. He will insult and inflict physical harm on his genitals or look for others to do so. The spirit of God cannot and will not be present when there is disrespect for the body of God.

Demonsapienism is a spiritual practice that True Cock Worshipers use to discern negative behavior. It helps them to know whom not to put their mouth on that mocks what they believe. Demans that do not care to recognize the presence of the sub-deity are shunned and are a waste of time. True Cock Worshipers are not fighters, but if they are cornered by an aggressive or violent volunteer they are required to surrender for a short period of time. Obviously there was no prior prayer or meditation.

Using a non-recommended volunteer could lead to spiritual warfare but an etkić might try to steer a servant of God away from making this bad decision. They see the dangers ahead and how it could distress a servant's spirit. Ultimately, it will always be a servant's decision whether to meet with an unworthy deman for oral practice.

When an ineligible volunteer already has been used for oral practice, the possibilities of an etūdame arriving shortly thereafter is the risk. Some etūdames like to believe that they are God's voice of reason and have the right to punish a True Cock Worshiper for ignoring the voice. Patiently, they will wait and then appear before the worn-out servant, usually preventing them from sleeping. These events can take place the moment a True Cock Worshiper is alone and about to sleep.

Facing an etūdame alone is the position that servants that do not pray or meditate can be placed in. Etūdames will shake and rattle the bed, and even scream into the ears of the servant until they are rudely awakened to deal with all alone. It is important to notify the ineligible volunteer that he cannot be used anymore due to spiritual conflict. This situation might end up becoming a damaged bridge if he is unable to accept or make sense of the reason, but life for him and the servant will go on.

When a volunteer does not deserve to be used, it does not mean that it is because of his penis. It could be because of any of the previous reasons mentioned. As soon as a volunteer believes he is doing you a favor cut him off and find another. Losing this kind of deman is a good thing. Do not feel guilty for walking away because he should have no problem removing himself from a non-sexual relationship. Do not be surprised if you are insulted for cutting him loose. Use this time to self-reflect on your demonic error and accept the consequences that follow.

There is nothing on this earth more disturbing than going down between the legs of a volunteer that thinks nothing of the sub-deity. True Cock Worshipers hate not having sexual domination and hate using volunteers that think only of their own needs when the spirit of the sub-deity is not present. Knowing that the spirit of the sub-deity is not present is the most depressing experience for a True Cock Worshiper.

Typical Cock Worshipers have no problem feasting in the territory of a deman that disrespects his own genitalia. There are little or no rules for Typical Cock Worshipers. They love teasing and insulting penises when given the opportunity.

The most common deman will challenge a servant's oral skills. Demans will often ask a servant to demonstrate their oral abilities. They believe True Cock Worshipers exist only to service them and that they are in the presence of a professional cocksucker. Ironically, volunteers actually do have the right to critique because the servant is there for oral practice and sometimes will ask for oral instruction. Although most demans in general believe they have the right to interrupt a session by making special requests, they cannot unless asked.

Being used for oral sex is all that matters to most volunteers. Unfortunately, they believe that everyone who sucks a cock is a True Cock Worshiper. They might not mock a servant of God's belief but they do not understand or care about it. True Cock Worshipers should therefore keep their conversations limited when in the environment of a selfish deman.

Be leery of clingy volunteers because they might end up becoming obsessed or a pest after a semi-cock worship session. Even after experiencing one-third of a worship session, or in other words a blowjob, they could become dangerous. Do not accept drinks, food, or gifts from volunteers. It is best to avoid getting close to them because they have the greatest potential to cause the most harm. This type of deman can become jealous and possessive. They have the greatest potential to stalk and terrorize and often have a mental illness. It is wise not to use them for a servant's own safety, but if so, do expect consequences.

Overly confident and dominant volunteers are red flags. They are the well endowed and confident peacocks of all demans. Their attitude is completely unpromising. They also have the natural pleasure to try and belittle a servant with intimidation. These demans have a suaveness that is repulsive to most servants of God. Their arrogance is usually a big turn off but they too are used for oral practice. Encounters with these demans might be limited to one time but then never again.

Overall, volunteers are generally not worthy of God's good air, but they are needed when there is no recipient. They might not ever become worthy of True Cock Worship, but they are still used for oral practice.

Sharing the details of penile rituals with anyone, especially volunteers, can lead to ridicule and mockery. They do not need to know about penile rituals no matter how often they ask. Most likely, a volunteer will never experience it, therefore it should be kept secret from them. It is pertinent that a True Cock Worshiper never demonstrate or discuss penile rituals with anyone other than their recipient. Praying ahead of time enables the servant to know whether a volunteer has the potential to become verbally offensive. They should never brag about their oral techniques nor should they mention rituals. Their mental state must be strong, humble and able to endure criticism from all directions.

Not many True Cock Worshipers will want to reveal their spiritual side with volunteers, and it is understandable as to why. Volunteers generally show sexually demonic traits that suggest, sex is the only thing they want. They have no interest for anything other than sex and show no (or very little) interest in a servant's beliefs. It explains why True Cock Worshipers will give a deman what he believes is the best blowjob he has ever had, then kick him to the curb. Volunteers are useful but more than often they have a disappointing mentality, making wanting them furthermore very difficult.

Servants are known to take charge and speak very little. They first will lay down the rules by telling a deman not to speak during a session and not to touch or help them. They will leave without finishing if he so much as picks up a cell phone at any time during a session.

His responsibility is to simply enjoy the moment without having to worry about telling the most famous lie, "I'll call you." It does not matter if a volunteer understands True Cock Worship or not, but he must have respect for the servant regardless.

Becoming the volunteer of a servant of God might be a deman's dream come true, especially when he is made aware of the potential benefits. It is as simple as waiting around for a call, text, or email notifying when and where he needs to be. When a volunteer knows that he is only being used for spiritual purposes, he will respect the servant for his own selfishness. There is nothing wrong with selfishness so long as he is faithful and honest about his lifestyle.

Most volunteers start off first as strangers then become best kept secrets or sometimes great friends. If a True Cock

Worshiper chooses a stranger over a friend, it is most likely because he has prayed about this stranger prior to meeting them.

There are cases in which a True Cock Worshiper will fall short and take desperate measures to worship God. The risks are high, especially if he or she is spiritually immature to the practice. An inexperienced servant could find himself stepping into an unfamiliar territory with a volunteer. They are also more susceptible to worshiping the volunteer rather than the sub-deity. True Cock Worshipers must be prepared to deal with the possibilities of having both a dominant and aggressive deman.

Volunteers have their own issues. They will fight unspoken battles of masculinity when it is not necessary. He might believe that the size of his cock is the primary intent for being used. Plenty of them will mock their own cock thinking it is less than adequate. A deman should understand that he has nothing to prove to a True Cock Worshiper in regards to the size of his penis.

It is inexcusable to say, "I was thinking with the wrong head." There is no such thing as, "thinking with the wrong head" according to True Cock Worship. The only two kinds of heads that both Demonsapienists and True Cock Worshipers believe in are the Godhead of our universe (figuratively speaking), and the head on our shoulders called "mentality."

Some volunteers might have a significant other. They are usually very ignorant about the concept of True Cock Worship. If a volunteer has a partner that does not understand or respect the beliefs of the servant, he or she never can be present during a semi-cock worship session.

Volunteers do not have the right to invite guests or visitors for learning and note taking. Time is not to be shared with a non-believer especially when they do not know the difference between religious practice and prostitution. If a volunteer's partner can prove that they know and understand the spiritual side of Demonsapienism and/or practices True Cock Worship, they can be present. When a deman believes that he has the right to have an uninvited guest for oral practice, immediately discredit and discard him.

A volunteer is around as long as he is respectful of the servant's needs. Usually True Cock Worshipers can tell after their first session if a volunteer is right for a long-term commitment. A volunteer is simply a volunteer because their requirements are not as stringent as that of a recipient. They will not be treated as a recipient due to their lack of qualifications. The journey for a volunteer engaging with a True Cock Worshiper sometimes comes with limitations or an expiration.

There is no rule against sexual intercourse, anal sex, or kissing when a True Cock Worshiper is not in the act of semi-cock worship. However, a volunteer never should forget that servants of God have a spiritual obligation that generally do not consider them for anything more than oral practice. True Cock Worshipers always will be in search of meeting the needs of an eligible and worthy recipient. If they find a recipient that meets the specified qualifications, then the volunteer will be disposed of.

Although a recipient is exactly what a True Cock Worshiper awaits, ending a long-term sexual relationship with a volunteer will be necessary. This arrangement should be reverted to a platonic state and not cut-off or it would be considered burning a bridge.

Recipients and volunteers are always eager about being sexually useful. However, they must remember not to overstep a True Cock Worshiper's boundaries. They must respect the servant and never try to tell him or her what to do.

All and all, whether a vessel keeper be a recipient or a volunteer, both might experience different stages of sexual bliss with a True Cock Worshiper during a worship session. An unspoken declaration of events might occur during worship sessions and can happen in various stages.

The first stage a vessel keeper has is to declare his commitment by surrendering his penis for an unlimited amount of time to help meet the needs of a True Cock Worshiper. He gives this charity willfully and honorably for the benefit of the servant.

The second stage is to have an unspoken declaration of emotional self-awareness through a long period of oral worship. A deman might find himself in tune with sexual pleasures that elevate him to an enlightenment in which he can recognize the spirit of the sub-deity. True Cock Worshipers will know when a recipient or volunteer has reached this crucial stage through meditation. This remarkable vision will become as clear as a glass of water for the servant of God. Recipients and volunteers usually do not experience this stage until after four or five cock worshiping sessions, if at all. This stage is not common; in fact, a servant might experience this particular spiritual accord with another deman only once or twice in a lifetime.

The third stage a vessel keeper has is his unspoken declaration that he, too, has connected with his penis in the same spiritual sense as has the servant of God. This stage is uncommon, but True Cock Worshipers know that these demans do exist.

The fourth stage of a vessel keeper's unspoken declaration is becoming mentally and spiritually discombobulated in the middle of a worship session. A deman can wind up drunk simply by the releasing of his toxins. He might lose visual perception or even become mesmerized by the servant of God's sensational skills.

The fifth stage of a vessel keeper's unspoken declaration is when he has managed a way to physically disassociate himself from the sexual act by meditating with the servant. When he is able to do this, he indeed will be rewarded by the omnipotent creator. This kind of experience might change his life forever, and he will be addicted. Any deman coming from out of this state of mind changes, for the experience is unforgettable. It is a solemn and most spiritual time where he can genuinely love himself. A deman might not ever admit it, but he cannot have a one-time oral experience after he has been with a True Cock Worshiper.

Chapter 13
SPECIAL AND UNIQUE SEXES

True Cock Worship is a non-discriminating, genderless belief that is set upon maintaining a structure of spiritual and mental stability for all. Demonsapienists believe that God created only one type of demon with two sexual distinctions; however, some demons come with rare exceptions. Most of us were born with one genital, whereas some demons were born with one of each and have two sub-deities. It does not get any better than this. The intersexed are by far the most fascinating of all demonsapiens, whether anyone wants to admit to it or not. They are said to be the most perfect of all Shem's creation.

Intersexed individuals are the most desired for True Cock Worshipers because they are believed to be closest to the physical identity of God, Shemself. The intersexed always will be born more complete than the common demonsapien. Unfortunately, they will also continue to fall victim to many medical demonic errors, and this is a crime. They have been used as science projects for as long as the medical profession has been around. They have been demoralized by the use of unnecessary experiments with the permission of demonsapien parents.

Biologically there are variations of intersexed individuals that Shem blessed to have with both male and female genitals. True Cock Worshipers therefore believe that the intersexed are the most adored by the creator of all things. Unfortunately in the first Dimension of Demonic Existence, commonly known as earth, the intersexed do not get the positive acknowledgment that they deserve. Most often demon parents will make the decision to hide this great blessing. They have been taught that it is a curse or an abnormal deformity. Whoever takes away an intersexed individual's right to decide whether to keep both genitals, insults the God that created everything.

After a demon has successfully completed three chanders, they could find themselves randomly selected to return as an intersexed individual, through the third Dimension of Demonic Existence. Many of them will return naturally weaker than most, due to the fact that they will be burdened with physical complications that often lead to psychological obstacles.

God created the intersexed as a way of demonstrating that Shem's most rare are Shem's best. Although unaware, the intersexed are far superior to all other living demons.

Marrying someone who is intersexed is the greatest blessing and gift on the earth, especially when they are able to help procreate. If a servant of God ever has the privilege of experiencing an intersexed demon, they should count their blessings and worship their genitals to no end.

Being born with two of the same parts is just as much a blessing. If you ever meet or have the honor of being in a relationship with a demon that has two of the same genitals, do your best to respect this individual and equally worship both genitals. A demonsapien born of true diphallus is like finding God Shemself.

If a mentally stable deman, with two penises, wants to become your life partner then you should give your soul to him. Thank God for bringing him into your life because they and the intersexed are the only exceptions to the rule for demonic worship. Thrones should be built just for the true diphallic and the intersexed to sit on to receive praises.

Chapter 14
ANIMALS AND WORSHIP

After going through the sexual reproduction process (also known as the third Dimension of Demonic Existence) and choosing to be an animal (the third Divinity of Demonic Evolution), demonsapiens always will be left to deal with the end result. To put it nicely, demon against beast is most fascinating for the reason that both want to eat one another. What to do with the beast is up to one's discretion; whether or not to worship or to eat it.

Demonsapienists believe that animals have an arrangement with God as well as everything else that Shem created. Demons that have passed through the third Dimension of Demonic Existence are living creatures among us. These demonic creatures have a new beginning but always end up having very little control of their earthly destiny. Becoming a domesticated animal and solely dependent on the cares of a demonsapien is risky. Domesticated creatures need our companionship just as we look to them for the same.

Some of us have a liking for demonic creatures that resemble the shape of a penis such as snakes, ferrets, eels, etc. There is something very forbidden and dangerous when becoming attracted to such creatures. There is a love-hate relationship with everything in this life. Shem had a perfect plan for everything that was created and put on earth.

God gave demonsapiens the liberty to become attracted to ALL things. We easily can desire the need to own a snake just because of the way it moves and feels. A snake is just like a penis. A snake can be either loved or eaten by any demonsapien that appreciates the very essence and delicacy of this beast.

The nature of most demonic creatures is to dominate what they can as a means for survival. Both demonsapiens and demonic creatures exhibit the same story of slaughtering and sexual reproduction for survival. God planted the same sexual desires that both the etkić and etūdames have when choosing to return as demonic creatures.

It might seem brilliant to return as an animal for the reason that an animal is not judged for being promiscuous, it is also a great risk. For example, True Cock Worshipers will study the mentality of a deman the same way one might study the venom from a poisonous snake. Demans become one in the same as the poisonous venom is his mentality. Snakes, as well as other animals, are known to lash out and bite even when nothing has provoked them. Harming another demon is not impressive.

When looking at all the demonic creatures of life, one has to come to the realization that the God of this universe brilliantly created them. The body of a snake, being God, is powerful and beautiful like that of the penis between a deman's legs. His cock is a creation of God's flesh for all demonsapiens to adore and respect.

Just as demonic creatures resembling the penis do not appear feminine in any way, it can be the same with a True Cock Worshiping demonica. She too can be both masculine and powerful yet beautiful and exotic in her own right, if she chooses.

Chapter 15
LUST AND LIVING SINGLE

God created love as well as hate, and while it is obvious that we as demons know how to hate, God would be pleased to witness each demonsapien applying the love that Shem created. It is an unusual way for many of us to live but, it makes sense when looking at it from a spiritual and realistic standpoint.

Like everything good in this life, there is also a negative side and a consequence for those who never seek God through all that was created. Oftentimes, demonsapiens prefer to live according to set principles within an organized religion and consequently live very depressing lives. The spiritually un-rested will inflict pain upon themselves as a means for punishment. Denial of lust also calls for others to choose a lonely life rather than sharing it on all levels by trusting other demonsapiens. A demonic match is not suppose to be perfect, just simply suitable. We have the potential to be fond of and care for another demon, which is the beauty to our journey in this life.

Getting seriously involved with a True Cock Worshiper is not going to be easy for any individual with a penis. A servant of God has to risk losing volunteers just to be in a commitment with one deman. It is best not to expect a True Cock Worshiper to settle into a monogamous relationship, especially if he or she has several demans committed and faithful to the cause.

A demon that attempts to take a True Cock Worshiper away from his or her recipient or volunteers might end up abandoned in the end. There is very little a deman can do to make a servant of God commit to one individual. However, the deman that is able to capture the interest of a True Cock Worshiper must have all the qualities that every volunteer and recipient requires. This is a very huge and demanding expectation that not many demans will be able to accomplish. A deman with selfish needs is more prone to being hurt if he is expecting to change a True Cock Worshiper.

Developing a natural inhuman resilience caused by emotional abandonment is a servant's way of adapting whereas; Typical Cock Worshipers are more inclined to struggle with emotional dependency. Love (lust) and acceptance is the most selfish expectation to put on a deman. Typical Cock Worshiping demonicas especially have this problem after only knowing a deman for a short period of time. They are more than likely to experience aggression after placing expectations immediately on a deman, after a successful encounter.

On the other hand, True Cock Worshipers are perfectly ideal for those that prefer a lifestyle free of relationship obligations. Those that do not want relationships get exactly what they need, while a servant is dedicated to being close to the lesser god.

True Cock Worshipers are strict not to develop an emotional attachment with their recipient or volunteer(s). Finding an ideal companion is always a challenge since a servant's spiritual belief is never easy to explain, especially with those that have very conservative views. The way to develop a relationship with a True Cock Worshiper is by respecting every element that comes with their belief. Although it can happen, servants of God will try their best not to cling to a recipient or volunteer for the risk of being led astray from Shem. If a relationship develops, it is usually after a recipient or volunteer has learned the concept of Demonsapienism. True Cock Worshipers are known for taking the dominant position, but will allow flexibility while in a relationship.

Sex with a True Cock Worshiper might not always be what a vessel keeper would expect as they are not always high-strung sex addicts like most might assume. This title might make them appear as cock-sucking fiends, ready to go hog-wild in the bedroom, but this assumption is very unrealistic. If you decide to go into a relationship with a True Cock Worshiper, just be aware that they are not porn stars or sex addicts.

Demonsapiens also have a breeding age deadline and an expiration date for connecting successfully with other demonsapiens. The age expiration for a handsome deman is forty-eight, which is why they should begin their search for mating immediately.

In the United States, after a demonica passes the Age of Forgiveness, the eyes of most demans will abandon her, no longer finding her attractive. Her Age of Deception ends at twenty-six. She has up until the age of forty-two to find a companion to accept her as she is. If she has not found her own way and does not have the faith to believe in Demonsapienism as a last resort, this demonica most likely will die without sexual companionship.

True Cock Worship allows the opportunity for all demons to find a suitable match. Be careful not to compromise with those that are not compatible or you will hinder yourself from happiness. God represents love, and the only way we can experience love is to find it through the human genitals.

True Cock Worshipers do not consider their oral sessions to be sexual although they are. Oftentimes a demon has difficulty comprehending why the servant did not become emotionally attached after a so-called sexual encounter. A True Cock Worshiper's oral sessions are meant to be purely spiritual experiences and nothing more.

Demans might be perfectly capable at managing themselves, but they thirst for the water that gives, in the way that they want to be needed. A recipient or volunteer(s) is prone to becoming emotionally imbalanced because they are vulnerable after being used as a demonic sacrifice. Servants of God will often experience the softer side of them while in this state. He has the opportunity to self-reflect on how to improve his life during every oral engagement. It is also the point in which he might feel as though he is looking at himself or that he has met his match. These type of demans are likely to take their chances by seeking a relationship with a True Cock Worshiper. He might find it refreshing to know that he has found someone whom he can identify with and satisfy his needs.

The best thing a deman can do to establish a relationship with a servant of God is to be vulnerable and honest. A way to show humility is by bowing down to a dominant servant of God and literally kissing his or her feet. He can also talk about his struggles and inferiorities. This too will capture the natural affection of a True Cock Worshiper. A deman can contain his feelings or let go by sharing them with a servant. He can accept the fact that he is a deman that is not worthy of anything.

True servants of God do not have the right to judge or tell the secrets of another demonsapien, no matter what it is. They are slaves for the ultimate God that demons should feel safe about confiding in. True Cock Worshipers believe it is necessary to overlook a vessel keeper's feelings with every engagement. They pray for his wellbeing but make a point to forget about his feelings; concentrating on the sub-deity at all times.

Using a deman for oral practice or to worship the sub-deity, is all that matters to a True Cock Worshiper. They are easily able to remove themselves from the same battles that a Typical Cock Worshiper has.

It is important that demans in search of True Cock Worshipers test those that claim to be true. Most cock worshipers are just typical and are not true in the spiritual sense. Demonsapienism is only a true path for those who wish to confront and manage their demonic nature. You will not find this spiritual practice with a Typical Cock Worshiper because they are still bound and burdened by traditional paths. Only for this reason, they are not trustworthy. A demonsapien that professes to being a True Cock Worshiper but has never heard of Demonsapienism is an imposter. Those who are identified as imposters should be embarrassed.

Trying to establish a relationship with a True Cock Worshiper is difficult. Taking one out on a date is always a kind gesture, especially if your eligibility is still debatable. Servants of God take one day at a time, and every day is different. There might be a time in the life of a servant when there is no recipient. He or she might acquire as many as 10 or more volunteers. None of them are said to be special, but one deman might stand out more than the rest as being more favorable.

There are many complexities to being single in the life of a True Cock Worshiper. They live a very fruitful life and are both passive and aggressive individuals. True Cock Worshipers for the most part are dominant in nature. They are sexual predators not only for the love of God, but for the love of the penis.

True Cock Worshiping demonicas can be mistaken as homosexual demans trapped inside the body of a demonica. They are very strong minded. It is also said that some demonica servants of God match the same libido as a homosexual.

True Cock Worshiping demonicas believe that generally all demonicas are deceptive. A deman will always encounter a demonica that complains about everything. He is often confused by a True Cock Worshiping demonica's free spirit or callousness towards him. He easily can become attracted to her because she is not seeking a serious commitment. When a vessel keeper is convinced that a True Cock Worshiper is not seeking to take him for a financial ride, he will be comfortable with her. He is charming until realizing that he is not the only one in her life.

There always will be several vessel keepers waiting for an opportunity to become a recipient or a volunteer. If you ever have the privilege of meeting a True Cock Worshiper, expect him or her to have more than one acquaintance in their life. If the servant does not, then it is possible that he or she has found both a lover and a recipient all in one.

Although a volunteer might not be the only one in a servant's life, everyone is made to feel special. Volunteers always will be considered friends unless the servant agrees to have a relationship with one of them. This is not a guarantee, and most likely it will not be a monogamous relationship.

True Cock Worshipers that enter relationships are usually prepared to think on the "Demon to Demon" approach. For example when a deman has wandering eyes, this grants a servant the same right. Whatever it is that would naturally offend a Typical Cock Worshiper or the common demonsapien, he should feel liberated enough to do. True Cock Worshipers never abandon a relationship unless the deman is trying to hurt them mentally, physically, spiritually and/or financially.

Some servants of God are ready for commitment but do not have time for mental instability. They can be just as ruthless as the next demon. They are able to recognize when lust is mistaken for love. True Cock Worshipers have plenty of lust to give but it is primarily directed towards the penis.

Lust is usually the only emotion that a True Cock Worshiper will establish with most demonsapiens. Some demans have a difficult time accepting this truth. For some, knowing that they will never have the heart of a True Cock Worshiper is an ego crusher. He might not be as offended after realizing how serious a servant is committed to their faith. Especially, when he knows that he too, can benefit. Most often a vessel keeper will compromise by sharing the servant just to get sexual gratification.

Recipients are most ideal when they are not too intelligent, especially after one understands his rights. If he is cleaver, he might figure out a way to use his rights against a servant and reverse the roles. A True Cock Worshiper that grows fond of their recipient and enters a relationship with one, might approve by giving into submissiveness. This is the tricky part about being a dominant servant. A dominant servants role is to be dominant, but if the recipient is also dominant he might find a way to take charge.

True Cock Worshipers must not lose their position by allowing vessel keepers to have options. Dominant demans are not to have any rights because the moment he sees an opportunity, he will manipulate the situation to make it more suitable for himself. For example, a True Cock Worshiper can have a recipient that intentionally breaks a rule knowing he or she has no one else to use for worship. Depending on the reason for his error, he knows that he can no longer be a recipient. He only broke the rule just to have sex with the servant. If the chemistry is mutual, he might end up dominating because he is no longer the recipient.

It is not unheard of that a recipient propose marriage to a servant. There is no rule against it, but there must be a mutual chemistry that triggers this engagement. Chemistry is something that only the recipient and the servant of God will be able to understand and establish together. True Cock Worshipers must take precautions when making this life-changing decision. It could affect the spiritual obligation they have with the sub-deity. Everything changes in the spiritual sense, so a servant of God must take time to think and meditate on the logical reasons for marrying their recipient.

Chapter 16
RELATIONSHIPS, LOVE, AND MARRIAGE

It is not common for a True Cock Worshiper to worship another demonsapien because they are constantly at odds. There is but one entity of love that is eternal, and that is the love that God has for all of Shem's creation. The love of God is here on earth. However, it does not and cannot exist among demons without the spirit of the sub-deity. The only kind of love that demons understand is the love that anoints two or more individuals together through the presence of the sub-deity. The penis carries an eternal love that spiritually binds demons to having a sacred experience.

Demonsapienism & True Cock Worship

When a True Cock Worshiper finds himself falling into deep lust with a recipient or volunteer, they will have to further think about what they want from that deman and if it requires more of a commitment. Oftentimes a relationship already is established without the label, and it is best to keep it that way.

Demons in general have a right to be unfaithful. Certain things can trigger the desire to be unfaithful or at least contemplate it. There is nothing abnormal about this nature since we are all demonsapiens. Dishonesty is also a part of being a demon. One must strive as a demonsapien to change dishonesty as well as demonic denial.

In marriage, the penis does not have to be used for sex, but a demonsapien can still pray and worship it. The body of God does not have to be erect to be worshiped, nor should he be required to have an erection for marriage. The truth of the matter is that marriage defiles all of the benefits that True Cock Worshipers make available. The concept of marriage generally represents little to no significance with True Cock Worshipers.

In other words, they see no benefit in it. They do however respect the different views and opinions of others regarding marriage and of a different faith.

Demonsapienists believe that marriage and monogamy is just another type of conformity. Marriage for most demon Americans is considered to be emotional, spiritual, sexual, and/or financial torture. Most want to be free and without restrictions and that is why there are so many divorces. Demonsapiens never should have to feel obligated to prove their devotion by professing it through a public ceremony. The sanctity of two demons coming together is not guaranteed, therefore marriage is actually a way to further curse a good thing.

According to Demonsapienism, marriage was designed as a way to trap a deman (male demon). Typical Cock Worshiping demonicas, with the gift of entrapment, will capture a deman while rewarding herself successful bragging rights of stealing his identity. She slowly will work on tearing down his ego, which is considered a slow death for the deman. As he begins to lose his self-identity, she will continue to work at him until he has broken. It becomes the most successful demonic extermination of personal character.

We are taught that infidelity is not an option for either, but it should be. Getting married is an expensive game that is played for the wrong reasons more often than not. Typical Cock Worshiping demonicas are very aggressive when it comes to seeking out marriage. Many of them will stop at nothing to make another demonica jealous by outshining her in a white dress that should be the color of blood. Demonsapienism discourages traditional marriage and believes that demons should marry only if they have found a partner that believes in open relationships with raw, honest communication.

Servants of God that do marry usually end up marrying their recipient. Good recipients that become a True Cock Worshiper's significant other can end up being treated as a living god. Once a deman becomes a True Cock Worshiper's living god, it becomes a marriage that is not to be taken lightly. A servant that was once a servant of God, the omnipotent, is suddenly the servant of his or her spouse. The sad irony in this is that marrying a recipient means marrying someone who fits all the requirements, which makes it strictly a monogamous marriage.

The risk is only after the deman realizes that he has both a servant's heart and soul. They are required to do just about whatever the voice of reason them tells to do for him. It becomes an ugly twist of demonic fate when the servant no longer has dominion over their recipient. Once he realizes that he is the dominant one, he will become as a living god to serve and wait on hand and foot. A deman should never be worthy of this, but it is a demonic decision that a True Cock Worshiper decides. True Cock Worshipers should study and test this deman before marrying him.

All recipients are supposed to be submissive. Submissiveness might not be what many demans have in mind, but this is what most True Cock Worshipers want. Never accept his marriage proposal until he has passed your requirements.

True Cock Worshipers are great to befriend for many different reasons. They are fully supportive of gay and lesbian relationships as well as gay and lesbian marriages. A homosexual deman, for example, unlikely wants anything to do with a demonica, unless he is still in the closet. Rather than being dishonest and hurting an innocent demonsapien, he will seek out a True Cock Worshiping demonica; always demonstrating a public respect for her, while his secret is safe.

True Cock Worshiping demonicas might willingly marry an "in the closet" deman to protect him from persecution. She also might carry his child if the relationship between the two is healthy. A deman in the closet will have sexual intercourse with a True Cock Worshiping demonica by depositing his sperm naturally, only for the purpose of sexual reproduction.

Posing as his lover when in fact she is not looks good to American society. Servants of God that marry straight-acting

211

homosexuals are entitled to practice their belief without interruptions. They might even share the lifestyle and practice True Cock Worship together.

True Cock Worshipers, whether gay, straight, or bisexual, do not believe in abandoning the penis. All True Cock Worshipers value the penis and look to it as a great blessing. It is therefore not supported when a demonica seeks artificial insemination or other such approaches to avoid the cock.

With that said, the same applies to True Cock Worshiping demonicas with lesbian lovers. There is no such thing as a True Cock Worshiping lesbian, but there is such a thing as a True Cock Worshiping bisexual. This is a rare group, but such individuals do exist. They know that for them to procreate or make a family, she must have a cock in her life in the real sense. Just as a closet deman requires heterosexual intimacy for a child, True Cock Worshiping demonicas gladly follow this process through natural intercourse.

Overall, marriage can be a unique arrangement within Demonsapienism when it is made into a business arrangement. Most Demonsapienists prefer not to marry. However if they do, it would be just to honor a family tradition and not considered a demonic error. A wedding ceremony is usually to cater to demonsapien family members of a different faith.

In closing, there will always be an underlying mentality of disagreement in the United States regarding True Cock Worship but Demonsapienism is suitable for all.

AN ODE TO DEMONSAPIENISM

I Believe There is a God

I believe I have been created by God.

But I am responsible for my own destiny.

I believe there is a God for more than one universe.

I believe there is a God over each of these universes.

I believe that I can have my own universe

if I care for an eligible recipient until death.

I believe the God who created us expects sexual entertainment.

We can discover God's spirit through the sub-deity which

rests between the legs of an eligible vessel keeper.

I do not believe in a place called Heaven or Hell.

I will not be defeated by the conformities of this world.

I will practice my faith in the way that represents a Demonsapienist.

I accept that I am a demon who wants to please the God of this universe.

If I stand alone in this faith, so be it.

I will be more alive in the next life and will return if I do not succeed.

By Lordess Demonica Copyright ©2009

Great God

Oh Great God! I cannot live without you!

I am thankful you are in the flesh and for my body.

I am thankful to consume you by oxygen and taste.

You are the very breath I take.

You are always in my thoughts.

Even when I am most distressed,

visions of your body comfort me.

When there is no one, I think of you.

And I am complete with these visions.

I feel whole when you are inside.

I will forever lift you up with praises!

There is nothing greater in this life.

You are forever in my soul Great Penis, Great God.

Amen

By Lordess Demonica Copyright ©2006

Penis Prayer
(Full Metal Jacket Inspired)

This penis is my God.

There are many like it but this one is mine.

My penis is my best friend.

It is my life.

I must master it as I must master my life.

Without God, my penis is useless.

Without my penis, I am useless.

I must respect my penis forever.

I must stiffen harder than my enemy, who is trying to belittle me.

I must submit to humility before God curses me.

I will.

Before God, I swear this creed:

my penis and I are defenders of breeding,

we are the masters of our destiny,

we are the saviors of this life.

So be it, until there is no humanity,

but peace.

Amen

By Lordess Demonica Copyright ©2007

GLOSSARY

THE GLOSSARY OF DEMONSAPIENISM

Age of Deception   A female that looks younger than 26

Age of Forgiveness   A female that is no older than 42

BDSM   Bondage, dominance, sadomasochism, masochism

Chander   A completion of three lifetimes on earth by the experience of one of the Three Divinities of Demonic Evolution

Cock Worship   Performing oral sex on a penis

Cock Worshiper   A generalized term used to describe someone who likes to give attention to the penis

Cultured Suppression To be emotionally, psychologically, financially, or spiritually controlled by a governing hierarchy in power

Deity   A god or goddess; of divine status

Deman   A male demon

Demon   Typically defined as, an unclean, malicious, and evil spirit; a physical entity that looks human but sometimes appears in its "true identity"; does not have a conscious or the concern to care for the good of anything. A generalized term used to describe both living and dead entities.

Demon to Demon   Treating someone in the same way they treat you; also known as an eye for an eye

Demonic Pollution   A demonsapien that builds his or her belief system solely on the knowledge that comes from another demon; having a faith or belief that originates from someone else

Demonic Prodigy   A demonsapien with the gift of knowledge and was used as an instrument on earth to enlighten other demonsapiens; the key to life for all or most demons; a demonic seed of knowledge that comes and goes with the unique ability to make the world agree; a famous genius

Demonica   A female demon

Demonnation   A formed organization of demons that agree upon the concept of their origins and what or who God is

Demonologist   One who believes in demons and seeks to learn about them

Demonology   The study of demons; the belief in worshiping demons

Demonsapien   A living demon that resides on earth in the embodiment of a human

Demonsapienism   The belief that all humans are demons; believing that all humans have demonic characteristics and are only civilized by cultured suppression

Demonsapienist   An individual that believes that all humans are demons; believing in the philosophy of Demonsapienism

Demonsapienology   The study of Demonsapienism

Docking   An uncircumcised deman masturbating another deman's penis with his foreskin

Dominant Servant   A True Cock Worshiper that is 100% in control of a worship session; the one that conducts sex without the interest of pleasing the one who is being serviced

Demonsapienism & True Cock Worship

Etkić   A dead demon from the second Dimension of Demonic Existence that returns to earth to do good deeds; also known as angels in other faiths

Etūdame   A dead demon from the second Dimension of Demonic Existence that returns to earth to cause harm on the living

Free Thinker   Someone that may/may not have discovered their own personal revelation but is following their own intellectual path

Gender   A category in which one is labeled or considered a female or male

Great Penis   A polite way to address the penis; showing respect for the penis

Hoe   A demon that quotes and/or studies the philosophy of both dead and living demons; appearing highly intellectual based on cultured philosophy; having very little intellectual substance of your own

Homo sapien   Mankind; a human being; a person

Humiliatrix   An individual that is primarily used for the purpose to humiliate or abuse sexually

Intellectual Path   The spiritual connection that binds an individual to God that no one else can define or discover but him or her

Irrumation   Aggressively and forcefully thrusting the penis into the mouth of another individual

Lesser God   A polite way to address the penis; showing respect for the penis

Penis   The genital organ of the male species

Personal Revelation	One's own mental, physical, and/or spiritual logic that is true and sacred to them but different to others
Quadruality	Four elements of God beginning with God, Shemself being the 1st, the sub-deity 2nd, the Voice of Reason 3rd, and the penis is the 4th element; all acting as one body in separate parts
Recipient	An eligible but submissive individual that is not necessarily a believer of True Cock Worship; someone willing to share his or her genitals with a True Cock Worshiper so he or she can connect with the sub-deity
Semi-Cock Worship	Having an intimate connection with the sub-deity, the spirit of God; oral worship without rituals; what volunteers are eligible for
Servant of God	Another term that describes a True Cock Worshiper
Sexorexia	To deprive oneself from having sex
Sub-Deity	God's spirit that can only be manifested in the flesh of a penis
TCE	True Cock Extremist
TCM	True Cock Moderate
TCW	True Cock Worshiper
True Cock Worship	Having an intimate connection with the sub-deity, the spirit of God; oral worship with rituals; only for recipients
True Cock Worshiper	One who literally believes in worshiping the penis spiritually, mentally, and orally; an individual that believes that some penises have the spirit of God

True Intelligence
Having the ability to think apart from everyone else through one's own personal revelation; having a broad combination of unique beliefs that are set apart from the rest

True Salvation
An individual that becomes sexually uninhibited and liberated without guilt or shame; being set free from religious conformity and taught beliefs that were once instilled as a child

Typical
One that follows the safe route or mainstream way of doing and/or thinking

Typical Cock Worshiper
One who enjoys performing oral sex and does not see the penis as a deity

Urethral Sounding
Stimulation of the prostate gland by using medical probes

Vessel Keeper
An individual born with genitals

Voice or Reason
Tapping into one's logic through communicating with God; common sense that is given to us directly from God

Weak Surface
Not having the ability to generate one's own spiritual knowledge without the influence of demonic pollution

Wee
A demon child or infant

Worship
Having the ability to commit one's life to a belief and/or devotion to a deity; having the interest to put solely whatever it is before everything else

TESTS AND QUIZZES

TEST 1

Am I a Typical Cock Worshiper or a True Cock Worshiper?

1. I have the tendency to get with those who have cocks over 6 ½ inches.   True False
2. I look for those who want oral sex.   True False
3. All I care about is making someone happy.   True False
4. I feel like going out and meeting someone. True False
5. I can stare for hours at penis photos that belong to strangers.

                                               True False
6. I might use a friend for sex.   True False
7. As long as I get sex from a man, it is all good.   True False
8. There is nothing more rewarding than to turn on someone who has a cock.   True False
9. I love making men ejaculate.   True False
10. Demans with low self-esteem are best for cock worship.   True False

Answers on page 232 and 233

225

QUIZ 1

Am I an Eligible Volunteer for a semi-cock worship?

1. I have a friend that likes to worship my cock.   Yes No
2. I cannot help but touch the one who is giving me head. Yes No
3. All I want is a blowjob and that is all.   Ye s No
4. I sit on my slave's face during blowjobs and hope that he or she vomits.   Yes No
5. I do not care what people's religious beliefs are.   Yes No
6. Anyone who gives a good blowjob is obviously a cock worshiper.

    Yes No
7. I am always ready to receive oral just tell me when.   Yes No
8. I am single and desperate for someone to suck on my cock.

    Yes No
9. I am in a relationship. A blowjob with a friend will have to be quick.   Yes No
10. I am pretty well endowed so it will take a lot to satisfy me orally.

    Yes No
11. My time is very valuable but I can set a date and a time for oral sex.

    Yes No
12. I jack off a lot because no one else will do it.   Yes No
13. Getting married is the last thing on my mind.   Yes No
14. It is not a good blowjob unless it is a throat fuck.   Yes No
15. I just want to get a blowjob drama free.   Yes No
16. I am uncomfortable with long-term commitments.   Yes No
17. I do not think my penis is attractive.   Yes No

18. I believe in open relationships where everyone is on the same page.   Yes No

19. The best blowjobs are the ones where I can cum in his or her mouth.   Yes No

20. A bad blowjob is when they just lick around the head.

Yes No

Answers on page 233 and 234

QUIZ 2

Am I an Eligible Recipient for True Cock Worship? Take the Quiz.

1.)   I have a friend that I use for sex and also likes to worship my cock.

                                                                Yes No

2.)   I cannot help but touch the one who is giving me head. Yes No

3.)   All I want is a blowjob and that is all.   Yes No

4.)   I am conservative when it comes to sex.   Yes No

5.)   I do not care what people's religious beliefs are.   Yes No

6.)   Anyone who gives a good blowjob is obviously a cock worshiper.

                                                                Yes No

7.)   I am always ready to receive oral just tell me when. Yes No

8.)   I am not much for giving, but I love receiving.   Yes No

9.)   I am in a relationship. A blowjob with a friend will have to be
      quick.   Yes No

10.) I am pretty well endowed so it will take a lot to satisfy me orally.

                                                                Yes No

11.) My time is very valuable but I can set a date and a time for oral sex.

                                                                Yes No

12.) I wish I could find someone to take care of my penis. Yes No

13.) Getting married is something important to me.   Yes No

14.) I prefer to spend quality time with one person.   Yes No

15.) I value my space and privacy but enjoy time with someone special.

                                                                Yes No

16.) I am looking for a long-term commitment.   Yes   No

17.) I do not think my penis is attractive.   Yes   No

18.) I believe in open relationships where everyone is on the same page.

     Yes   No

19.) The best blowjobs are the ones where I can cum in his or her mouth.   Yes   No

20.) A bad blowjob is when they just lick around the head.   Yes   No

Answers on page 234 and 235

TEST 2

Am I A Demonsapienist?

1.) I believe in something called the quadruality.   True False

2.) Some of us are demons.   True False

3.) We are all just demons living in attractive skins.   True False

4.) I am a Demonsapienist and I also attend a Christian church.

    True False

5.) I became a Demonsapienist because I believe in worshiping demons.   True False

6.) Aliens come from other planets within this universe.   True False

7.) I became a Demonsapienist because I am a demonsapien.

    True False

8.) There is a demonic hierarchy of angels like Gabriel.   True False

9.) Demons are related to aliens.   True False

10.) I am a Demonsapienist that loves to suck cock therefore, that makes me a True Cock Worshiper.   True False

11.) The human genitals are an extension of God.   True False

12.) There is a place called purgatory after death.   True False

13.) Demonsapienism teaches True Cock Worshipers how to live for God.   True False

14.) I am a Demonsapienist because I do not believe in religious conformity.   True False

15.) If you stand up to an etūdame, the spirit world will respect you.

    True False

16.) There are other universes beyond ours.   True False

17.) I have no problem calling someone's newborn a demon child.

                                                              True False

18.) Demonic error is another term that references to sin.   True False

19.) Demonsapiens live in one of the Three Dimensions of Demonic
    Existence.   True False

20.) God is intersexed therefore; we can refer to him as she or he.

                                                              True False

Answers on page 236 and 237

TEST 1

Answers from page 224

1.) True. You focus on the size of the penis.

2.) True. You are seeking to satisfy.

3.) True. You are focused on meeting the needs of others.

4.) True. You are seeking physical chemistry.

5.) False. A real penis is what captures your interest.

6.) True. You are seeking physical chemistry.

7.) True. You are focused on your needs and meeting the needs of others.

8.) True. You are focused on meeting the needs of others.

9.) True. You are focused on meeting the needs of others.

10.) False. You prefer to have someone dominate you.

A Typical Cock Worshiper would have answered at least one question correctly.

TEST 1

Answers page 224

1.) False. Size is not relevant.

2.) False. Oral sex is not on your top list of obligations.

3.) False. True Cock Worship is not about fulfilling a deman's sexual needs but rather his emotional needs.

4.) False. You are contacted for meeting emotional connections.

5.) True. It is a form of prayer and meditation.

6.) True. This would only be for personal needs and not True Cock Worship.

7.) False. True Cock Worshipers do not seek self-gratification through oral worship.

8.) False. True Cock Worship is not about fulfilling a deman's sexual needs.

9.) False. True Cock Worship is not about helping demans to achieve sexual satisfaction

10.) True. Part of being a True Cock Worshiper is dedicating one's self to meeting the emotional needs of pitiful demans.

In order to be considered a True Cock Worshiper, <u>ALL</u> 10 questions must have been answered correctly.

QUIZ 1

Answers from pages 226 and 227

1.) Yes. However, sexual intercourse is usually not permitted unless it is consensual.

2.) Yes. It is only permitted if the decision is equally mutual.

3.) Yes. A volunteer that does not have high expectations is ideal.

4.) Yes. This is only permitted if the True Cock Worshiper makes a request for it.

5.) Yes. A volunteer should only be concerned about his own belief.

6.) No. True Cock Worshipers do not believe that just anyone is a cock worshiper.

7.) Yes. A volunteer with this mindset might be used several times a day.

8.) Yes. You will love being used as a demonic sacrifice to God.

9.) No. True Cock Worshipers spend hours with the sub-deity. Patience is expected until the servant is finished.

10.) Yes. You are entitled to your opinion.

11.) No. True Cock Worshipers generally do not operate this way but they will adjust their schedule if you are the only volunteer.

12.) Yes. A True Cock Worshiper will naturally accommodate this dilemma.

13.) Yes. Not wanting to get married is your prerogative. True Cock Worshipers do not care about your fear of marriage.

14.) No. However, you are entitled to your opinion.

15.) Yes. This is a great attitude to have since you might not be the only volunteer.

16.) Yes. This is a great attitude to have since; you might be used only once.

17.) Yes. You are entitled to your opinion.

18.) Yes. This is a great attitude to have since you might not be the only volunteer.

19.) Yes. It is only permitted if the decision is equally mutual.

20.) Yes. You are entitled to your opinion.

You might be an **ELIGIBLE** volunteer if you answered YES to all of the questions except 6, 9, 11 and 14. You are **INELIGIBLE** if you answered yes to 6, 9, 11 and 14.

QUIZ 2

Answers from pages 228 and 229

1.) No. Sexual intercourse is not permitted when you are a recipient.

2.) No. Touching the servant of God is not permitted during a True Cock Worship session.

3.) Yes. A recipient is only used for oral.

4.) Yes. That is your prerogative.

5.) Yes. A recipient should only be concerned about his own religious belief.

6.) No. True Cock Worshipers do not believe just anyone is a cock worshiper.

7.) Yes. A recipient with this mindset might be used several times a day.

8.) Yes. You will love being used as a demonic sacrifice to God.

9.) No. True Cock Worshipers require long hours with the sub-deity. You would have to remain patient until the servant of God is finished.

10.) Yes. You are entitled to your opinion.

11.) No. True Cock Worshipers depend on the recipient for oral and may require them to be available at any time.

12.) Yes. If you are mentally stable, a True Cock Worshiper will take care of this dilemma.

13.) Yes. Wanting to get married is your prerogative.

14.) Yes. This is a great attitude to have.

15.) Yes. This is a great attitude to have.

16.) Yes. This is a great attitude to have since you will be the only one.

17.) Yes. You will be cared for as an eligible recipient if you feel this way.

18.) Yes. This is your prerogative and it is a good attitude to have as a recipient.

19.) Yes. You are entitled to your opinion.

20.) Yes. You are entitled to your opinion.

You might be an ELIGIBLE recipient if you answered YES to all of the questions accept: 1, 2, 6, 9 and 11. You are INELIGBLE if you answered YES to 1, 2, 6, 9 and 11.

TEST 2

Answers from pages 230 and 231

1.) TRUE. The quadruality is the foundation of Demonsapienism.

2.) FALSE. All humans are demons.

3.) TRUE. We are all demons living in attractive skins.

4.) TRUE. Demonsapienists attend places of worship as a form of entertainment. Unfortunately, they cannot bring popcorn with their visits.

5.) FALSE. Demonsapienists do not worship demons.

6.) FALSE. Aliens come from another universe outside and beyond our own.

7.) TRUE. This is the most logical reason for becoming a Demonsapienist.

8.) FALSE. There is no such thing as a hierarchy within the spirit world.

9.) TRUE. Demonsapienists believe that they are related to aliens.

10.) FALSE. A Demonsapienist is not automatically a True Cock Worshiper just because they like to suck cock.

11.) TRUE. The human genitals are an extension of God.

12.) FALSE. Demonsapienists do not believe in purgatory.

13.) TRUE. True Cock Worshipers learn to deal with other demons with the philosophy of Demonsapienism.

14.) TRUE. Demonsapienists hate organized and religious conformity.

15.) TRUE. You will earn the respect of other demonic entities if you can face them on your own.

16.) TRUE. Demonsapienists believe that there is an unknown level of universes, both above and below ours, in different dimensions.

17.) TRUE. Newborns are demons that will soon develop their own demonic nature.

18.) FALSE. There is no such thing as sin. Demonsapienists will however refer to sin in discussions to relate with narrow minded demons.

19.) TRUE. There are Three Dimensions of Demonic Existence. The one that demonsapiens reside on is the first dimension, also known as earth.

20.) FALSE. Demonsapienists refer to God as Shem, never she or he.

You can call yourself a Demonsapienist if you answered ALL of the questions correctly.

AUTOBIOGRAPHY

Demonsapienism is a belief that first originated out of North America by a demonsapien named Kia. She was attacked, and is still occasionally attacked, by other demonic entities. These demonic persuasions compelled her to acknowledge their existence and write about them.

Kia discovered her own personal revelation and this unique philosophy throughout demonic torment. Her sole desire was to describe the face of her reality as well as leave her legacy before death.

She calls for all Demonsapienists to come forward and honorably represent their demonic lineage. There is no secret of divine power and if so, Kia has unlocked the secrets of creation by saying that we are all demons with sexual desires.

DEMONSAPIEN®

Your information is secure while shopping on Zazzle. It is top priority to satisfy the customer. If you are not absolutely satisfied with your purchase, return it for a full exchange or refund within 30 days of receipt.

Contact Customer Support for an RMA (Return Merchandise Authorization) number. Write RMA on the packing slip in your return package. Return it to the following address:

Zazzle Inc.
Returns Department
1185 Campbell Ave.
San Jose, CA 95126

(1)	(2)	(3)	(4)

(5)	(6)	(7)	(8)

(1)	DEMONSAPIEN Coffee Mug	$13.95
(2)	DEMONSAPIEN Stainless Steele Drinking Cup	$20.95
(3)	DEMONSAPIEN Bumper Sticker	$ 4.45
(4)	DEMONSAPIEN, DEMON CHILD Tote Bag	$25.95
(5)	TRUE COCK WORSHIP (TCW) Key Chain	$16.95
(6)	DEMONSAPIEN Mouse Pad	$10.95
(7)	DEMONSAPIEN, DEMON CHILD Demonica T-Shirt	$20.95
(8)	DEMONSAPIEN Unisex Hooded Pullover	$34.95

www.zazzle.com/demonsapien

CONTACT LORDESS DEMONICA

www.truecockworship.com
lordessdemonica@gmail.com

PAPILIO PUBLISHING COMPANY
PO BOX 18595
INDIAN SPRINGS, NEVADA 89018-0139